WHATEVER IT TOOK

Kenneth LaMascus

STEPHENE F. AUSTIN STATE UNIVERSITY PRESS
NACOGDOCHES ✯ TEXAS

Copyright © 2014 by Kenneth LaMascus
All rights reserved. Printed in the United States of America.
No part of this book may be used or reproduced in any manner whatsoever without written permission except in the case of brief quotations embodied in critical articles or reviews.

For information address:
Stephen F. Austin State University Press,
1936 North Street, LAN 203
Nacogdoches, TX 75962

sfapress@sfasu.edu

Book Design: Andrea Laham and Troy Varvel
Cover photo: Steven LaMascus
Publisher's Note: The gun pictured on the cover is the one LaMascus carried from 1974 until his retirement

LIBRARY OF CONGRESS CATALOGING-IN-PUBLICATION DATA

Whatever it Took / Kenneth LaMascus—1st ed.
p.cm.
ISBN 978-1-62288-060-7

1. Border Patrol 2. Borderlands 3. Criminal Justice
4. Kenneth LaMascus 5. Title

First Edition: 2014

Contents

Introduction ★ 5
Biography ★ 7
Foreword ★ 9
Part One: Investigations and Deputy Sheriff ★ 11
Part Two: The U.S. Border Patrol ★ 71

★ Introduction ★

I've known Kenneth LaMascus for almost 30 years, and have known of him for much longer. He is a man of integrity, honesty, and subtle humor, someone modest to a fault, who doesn't brag or call undue attention to himself. I was lucky enough to work with him during the last years of his law enforcement career and I can say without hesitation that he is one of the best Agents I ever knew. No one worked harder, longer, or smarter than Kenneth, and he did it all with a joy and spirit that inspires me to this day. Kenneth's biography covers in excellent detail his exploits in rural law enforcement during a time that, although not so long ago, is an era we will never see again. It was a period of limited resources and sporadic or nonexistent communication where officers were forced to be highly independent and self-reliant in order to get the job done. It was that or they didn't last long. Kenneth's law enforcement career spanned more than three decades.

This book is written in words that mirror the man, and I am proud to say that man is my friend.

Billy Kring
Chief Patrol Agent (Ret.), U.S. Border Patrol

★ Biography ★

I was born August 23, 1929, in Chickasha, Oklahoma. Except for three years spent in New Mexico, I was raised in Garvin County, Oklahoma. My father was a farmer, and my mother was a school teacher. We lived in Cottonwood Community near Maysville, where Father farmed. After World War II broke out, Mother taught in the Cottonwood School and was teaching there when I finished eighth grade. I went to high school in Maysville the first year and then attended school at Elmore City the next three years where Mother taught school at the elementary school in the Parks Community.

I moved with the family to Nocona, Texas, in 1948, where Mother taught in the Prairie Valley School and my father took a job as custodian. I went to college that semester in Gainesville, Texas, then dropped out and worked at various jobs in the Nocona area, including oil field construction.

I married Sylvia Mowery in May of 1950 and took a job with Nocona Boot Company. By 1957, we had two sons and were expecting another in September of that year. I was working at the boot company and also at the local movie theater in order to give my family a decent standard of living.

I decided to leave both of these dead-end jobs and find something that would provide our family a better living than we had in the present situation. I first applied for employment with a major oil company and scored well on their aptitude test and was hired pending approval of their medical team. The doctors found something in my back they did not like and ruled that there was a high probability that my back would not hold up to the work.

This development caused me to look for work I would be better suited for. After some searching, I found an opening with a company which did general investigations. I liked what I learned from the personnel department of this company. I applied for employment, scored well on their tests, and was hired. After a training period in Fort Worth, Texas, I was assigned to work out of the Wichita Falls, Texas, office.

I was raised in rural Oklahoma, attended a rural community grade school and a small town high school, and was not inclined to move my family into a congested urban setting. I rented a house in Henrietta, Texas, and drove the 20 miles to the office in Wichita Falls. My oldest son, Steven, attended school his first year in Henrietta, but was walking several blocks to school. The next year, I rented a farm house near Petrolia, Texas. This was about the same distance from the office, and my son could ride a school bus from our house to school and back.

The next year, I got the opportunity to move to Seymour, Texas, and open a one-man office covering a large area in which Seymour was more or less centrally located. The nature of my investigative work with this company required me to check various records and contact area law enforcement agencies. I became acquainted with many law enforcement officers from the Denton and Gainesville areas in the East and the Quanah and Benjamin areas in the West. In Seymour, I worked out of an office in my home for some two years until I went to work as the deputy sheriff of Knox County at Benjamin, Texas.

★ Foreword ★

As a member of law enforcement, when making an investigation and attempting to get the information necessary to make a comprehensive report or a prosecutable criminal case, it sometimes becomes necessary to deviate from the routine. The methods I used and the lengths to which I would go in such a case were limited by only two things: the law and my personal code of ethics. The reader will find examples of my brand of law enforcement throughout this book. In one case, instead of observing traffic by parking my vehicle at the side of the road and observing the vehicles as they drove by, I hid my vehicle under a bridge and observed the passing traffic from a blind built of brush in the pasture near the bridge. This allowed my partner and me to accomplish a specific objective.

The same principle applied to making arrests. I worked alone much of the time and arrested thousands of people, many of whom were in groups. When approaching a person or persons with the intention of making an arrest, I tried to leave absolutely no doubt in anyone's mind as to who was in charge. When, in rare cases, physical resistance was encountered, the term "whatever it took" had to apply. There is no provision in the law whereby an officer is justified in failing to make an arrest simply because resistance is encountered.

If I had a secret, it was in always being right. I worked twenty-six years in law enforcement and never failed to affect an arrest once it was attempted. I was never sued, investigated or charged with violating anyone's civil rights. Although I had numerous close calls, including facing several men who were armed and would have gladly put a bullet into me or stabbed me with a knife, I was never forced to use my gun against anyone. I attribute this to being vigilant and being able to recognize and neutralize a situation before it came to that point. I will be the first to admit that good, old-fashioned luck may have also played a part in this.

I am sure many readers will notice that in describing some of the cases I did not follow procedure that would be required to meet today's standards. In 1961, when I began working in Knox County, Miranda was a fellow who worked at a service station in

Munday. The Arizona court case which lead to the requirement to warn a suspect of his rights against self-incrimination and became known as the Miranda Warning was not decided until 1966.

Some notable cases are not mentioned in this book. I will only say that there are a few cases that I will never be able to give a full, honest account of because to do so could cause repercussions for which I do not want to be responsible.

I drove county and federally owned vehicles many hundreds of thousands of miles. My vehicle accidents consisted of a few minor dents caused by things like swinging gates, deer, livestock, and such. I was never involved in an accident that resulted in any injury to me or a passenger, or in which the vehicle was damaged to the point that it was unusable.

Part One:

Investigations and Deputy Sheriff

★ Chapter One ★

Although this is written to highlight my career in law enforcement, I learned the basics of investigations, interviews, record checks and the various techniques used in law enforcement while employed by a company that did general investigations. Most of these investigations involved insurance, but many involved credit, personnel, and almost anything the requesting company wanted.

The investigations I made for this company took me over a large area in north Texas. I worked from the Lewisville, Denton, and Gainesville areas in the east, to the Quanah, Crowell, and Benjamin areas in the west, and as far south as Graham and Olney. During the latter part of this time, I lived in Seymour, worked out of my home and received a car allowance to cover travel expenses. I became acquainted with many of the people in law enforcement in this area. I usually had time for coffee, lunch, or just swapping stories with the people in law enforcement. I could also occasionally help officers in one jurisdiction locate a person they wanted who had fled their area. It was little trouble for me and greatly helped my standing with the law enforcement community. If the person in question had applied for credit, such as financing a car, renewing insurance or a number of other transactions, I could usually find a current address and job location through a check of our records. I was careful to maintain my contacts and used this ability to great advantage after going into law enforcement.

I handled a request in the Wichita Falls area for the investigation of a claim of disability from a man who claimed an injury to his ankle while working for a company building a new runway at Sheppard Air Force Base. I went to his house and interviewed the claimant. He was personable, smooth, and a good talker. While I was there, he got a phone call from a girlfriend and was telling her that a man was there all the way from Chicago to handle his injury claim. He handed the phone to me and said, "Talk to the woman." Well, the company who had ordered the investigation was a Chicago company, so I told the lady he was right.

The claim seemed legitimate. His foreman at Sheppard remembered the incident and said he did not personally see the accident, but did remember that it occurred early in the day. The claimant was pushing a load of concrete down a ramp, fell off, and injured his ankle. The foreman had gotten to the scene a few minutes later and found him being tended by fellow workers. The foreman said he had no reason to doubt the claim was legitimate. I had enough information to approve his claim, but a nagging feeling that something was amiss caused me to decide to check further.

I went to the courthouse to see what kind of fellow I was dealing with. I found nothing amiss until I got to the records of the sheriff's department where I found that sheriff's deputies raided a dice game on the second floor of a local building on the Saturday night before the man claimed his injury the following Monday morning. He had jumped out of a second story window to escape arrest and injured his ankle. He was arrested and taken to a local hospital emergency room where he had been treated and released back to the sheriff. I confirmed this with the hospital and then wrote a report which I am sure resulted in the cancellation of his ticket to ride the gravy train.

Another instance while I was doing this work was a case in Olney, Texas. I received a request to check with the hospital in Olney regarding a woman who had been diagnosed with cancer, and had undergone a radical mastectomy of both breasts. I received her records from the supervisor in charge of that department and, with him sitting across the desk from me, went through her case records. I could hardly believe what I had found. The biopsy report clearly found cancer, and breast removal was indicated; however, the post-operative examination of the tissue removed found not a trace of cancer.

The hospital could offer no explanation. The possibility that the biopsy had resulted in removal of all affected tissue seemed unlikely. The other possibility, that a mix up at the laboratory had resulted in the wrong test being attributed to this patient, seemed more likely. I elected not to alert the lab at that time and requested further authorization and directions before proceeding. I never heard anything else regarding this case and, consequently, the reason for the strange results in her file is still a mystery to me.

One incident in the investigating job involved a claim of injury by an insured person who was a member of a crew building a new, higher bridge across one of the many streams in the area. I no longer remember the name of the stream or the number of the road, but I do remember that it was an isolated area somewhere northwest of Seymour, Texas.

The insured was alleged to have fallen on, near, or from the bridge and suffered rather severe injuries. I found the site without difficulty. It was not much of a stream but it had an impressive gorge to cross. I parked with the crew's vehicles at the end of the bridge and looked for someone to talk to. I finally found a man working under the bridge on my side and asked him for the supervisor. He waved a hand vaguely toward the other side of the bridge.

I had noticed a crew of four or five men working about the middle of the span as I had arrived. I thanked him and started looking for a way to get to the crew working on the bridge. There were a few boards lying across the girders right at the end of the bridge, but this soon became a girder which seemed to me to be about six inches wide. I walked a few tentative steps on this girder or I-beam and stopped.

I looked down and discovered I was already 100 feet above ground and getting further with every step. I had never suffered from vertigo, but upon studying the situation for about 10 seconds, I decided there was no one out there that I wanted to see badly enough to walk the remaining fifty yards on that I-beam which was not much wider than my shoes. I carefully made my way back to the end and asked the fellow if he knew the insured. He informed me he was new and had just taken the place of a man who had been injured on the job there. I then inquired how long he thought it might be before the foreman came to the end. He told me it would not be soon because they had just started out there and had several I-beams to bolt together.

That was before handy-talkies were common and cell phones had not yet been invented. Well, the sun was low down in the west when the crew finally finished and came to the bank. I got my statement and finished my investigation. It was late and dinner was long past when I finally got home that day.

While living in Seymour, I conducted an investigation on a man who had lived in Knox County but had gone to the Dallas-Ft. Worth area and was being considered as a partner in a business deal with a group of investors in that area. They decided to check on his background before going into partnership with him in whatever venture was being considered. I talked with a couple of people who had done business with him and found he was a wheeler-dealer type with grandiose ideas, and they would not consider going into business with him if he was to have any part of managing said business. The last person I interviewed was president of the bank in the town where he had lived. When I mentioned his name, the banker brought forth a file and handed it to me. It detailed attempts by the bank to collect outstanding debt from the subject, and across the last page had been written "Deceased" and the outstanding debt column still showed a sizable balance. Since the fellow was clearly still alive, I looked at the banker and said "Deceased?" Without even the hint of a smile, the banker said, "As far as I'm concerned, the son of a bitch is dead." I wrote up my report listing the facts just as I found them. I never knew what the investors who ordered the report decided.

★ Chapter Two ★

I had one uncle who was a railroad detective with the Union Pacific railroad and worked out of Barstow, California. Another uncle was a highway patrolman in Nevada and worked out of Las Vegas. A third uncle had worked as a policeman in Las Vegas prior to returning to Oklahoma and buying the Jenkins' family farm from the other heirs after my Grandmother Jenkins had died. I grew up listening to stories of my uncles' adventures in their various fields of law enforcement. This probably influenced me to be receptive to the opportunity to go into law enforcement. While living in Seymour, I became friends with the sheriff and his deputy there in Baylor County and would occasionally ride with one of them when I was not too busy in my job. The more I saw of the work they were doing, the more inclined I was to look for an opportunity to get into law enforcement.

In 1961, Knox County Sheriff Homer T. Melton was appointed as a Texas Ranger and assigned to the Benjamin area. His deputy, H.C. Stone, was appointed sheriff for the unexpired term. This created a vacancy and Stone approached me about taking the job. The base salary was not sufficient to justify chang-ing, but Stone was able to offer me a contract to feed the prison-ers in the jail and to use the living quarters in the jail. This made the job economically feasible and I accepted the job. Although I had no law enforcement experience, the sheriff knew I was a competent investigator and able to handle correspondence and write reports. The sheriff hated paperwork and this arrangement proved to be a good one. We made a good team.

I moved my wife, three sons, and a daughter expected in a few months into the jail where we lived for the next six years. There was no academy or other training available so my training in law enforcement was to be strictly on the job. I was given a booklet of tickets and the sheriff loaned me a pistol until I could order one of my own. When I resigned to take an appointment as a U.S, Border Patrolman in 1967, I turned the ticket booklet back in. I had written a total of five or six tickets during my tenure as deputy. We did not consider ourselves traffic officers and if the offense observed did not justify an arrest, a verbal warning was usually sufficient.

Since there was no formal training available and I needed to know what the law was, I found the County Attorney's Office (next door to the sheriff's office) invaluable. I read Vernon's Annotated penal code, and also the Southwest Reporter, which is a record of both criminal and civil cases appealed from lower courts. I read these cases back to antiquity. One such case involved the theft of corn from a corn crib, and whether deadly force was justified to prevent the fruits of theft. The court ruled that deadly force could be used as long as the perpetrator was within gunshot range of the place where the theft occurred. I could imagine the farmer saying, "Ma, fetch me the sharps." It took a couple of months or so, but I soon had a good working knowledge of the law and how to enforce it.

When I was five years old, my father developed health problems and had to have surgery to have a tumor removed. The doctors recommended that he move to a higher, drier climate. As a result, he moved his family from Oklahoma to Tucumcari, New Mexico, where we lived for a time in a house rented from a man named Bullington, who was also mayor of the town. While living next to the Bullingtons, I met and played with their granddaughter, who was my age. I also met her cousin, a boy named Tom, whose parents lived in El Paso, but visited with the Bullingtons in Tucumcari every few months. During the three years we were in New Mexico, I saw and played with Tom several times. He was a couple of years older than me, but we got along well together.

Although I had frequently visited the Sheriff's Department when I was an investigator and living in Seymour, I had never met the County Attorney who, although he had an office in the court house in Benjamin, lived in Munday and had an office where he had a private law practice.

After I moved to Benjamin and started my job as Deputy

Sheriff, the day arrived when the county commissioners met for their regular monthly meeting and all the county officials were in their offices in the courthouse. The Sheriff introduced me around and when it came to my introduction to the county attorney, the Sheriff said, "Tom, this is my deputy, Kenneth LaMascus. Ken, this is the county attorney, Tom Bullington." It took a few seconds but we both realized we had known each other when we were kids. As a hard-nosed lawman and investigator, I was (and still am) skeptical of coincidences, but the odds of us coming together in this manner twenty-five years later and hundreds of miles away must be astronomical.

I soon found that Tom was a fine attorney and, although taking the county attorney job was a side line, was willing to take the time out of his regular practice to more than adequately take care of his duties for the county. I can't remember his ever refusing to take care of the needs of his office no matter what time of night or other circumstance.

Looking back over a 26-year career in law enforcement, I arrested thousands (yes, thousands) of persons, most of whom were illegal aliens in the U.S. One of the most dangerous of the lot happened early in my career when I was deputy sheriff in Knox County, Texas.

I was on patrol east of Benjamin (the County Seat) when I encountered four young men stopped at the side of the road. They were out of their vehicle relieving themselves, one in the middle of the highway. I stopped and talked to them and, while talking, noticed one was moving to my left away from the others. I told him to move back and one of them said he was a deaf-mute. I soon noticed him take another step and he appeared to be trying to get behind me or at least out of my line of sight. I asked the one who said the man was deaf if he could communicate with him. He said he could, so I told him to tell the man to get back with the group and that I would not tell him again.

It was a cold winter night and we were standing in my car lights. They were all in various states of intoxication, and I thought I could smell marijuana. I saw something slide from under his coat and hit the ground. One of them said something in Spanish which I did not speak or understand at that time, and they all ran.

I caught the one who had dropped what later proved to be a knife with a six inch blade. I caught him at the right-of-way fence, handcuffed him, and, while I was doing that, one of the others got back to their car and took off, picking up the other two some 50 yards up the road. I got the prisoner secure and started after the others who by that time had close to a minute head start.

As I came into Benjamin, I saw a local resident. I stopped and asked if he had seen the car I was following. He said it came through at high speed and almost ran him down, running without lights, and that it had gone on west toward Guthrie.

I resumed pursuit toward Guthrie some 30 miles away. There were no side roads they could see to take running without lights before they almost got into Guthrie. My vehicle was equipped with a cowl-mounted spotlight on the driver's side with a control I could operate while driving. I turned on the spotlight and settled in for however long it would take to overtake the vehicle. Since he was still running without lights, I could not see him, but was sure he was not much over a mile ahead. Some eight miles west of Benjamin, I saw a burst of light some one-half mile ahead of me and began slowing down from the 120 mph I was driving. The driver of the fleeing car could have seen that he was being overtaken and apparently was paying too much attention to his rearview mirror.

I found the fleeing vehicle against a pasture fence beginning to burn. It had hit the concrete abutment of a culvert at 100 mph. This ripped the underside out, ruptured the gas tank, and the sparks had ignited the gas. This was the burst of light I had seen. I never knew if there was marijuana in the car as it was badly burned before the fire department arrived. Two of the three were still at the scene, and I arrested them there. The driver had crossed the pasture fence and run away.

While waiting for the fire department to get the fire under control and an ambulance to arrive, an eastbound 18-wheeler stopped and delivered the escapee to me. The truck driver had been one of the drivers who had stopped and helped me get the scene under control. When other help arrived, the truck driver started on west but returned a few minutes later with the escapee. The truck driver had seen the man I had been chasing come to the road and try to catch a ride on west. Fortunately, he picked him up and brought him back to the scene. One was treated and released back to me from the hospital emergency room and all four spent some weeks in the county jail for various infractions of the law.

The first man arrested was innocuous in appearance. He was some 5 feet, 7 inches tall, 130 pounds. He was neither deaf nor mute. He could hear and speak as well as anyone. He, aided by a friend, used a ruse in an attempt to get behind me. When that failed, he dropped his knife and ran. He was a man who liked to use the knife. Record checks revealed he had a lengthy record and was out on bond for a knife attack in the Lubbock area. His bondsman was notified and elected to withdraw from his bond. I delivered him to his bondsman.

About a year later, I read in a DPS bulletin that he had been arrested in the Lubbock area for stabbing a constable at a dance. I still have the knife he dropped and, through the remainder of my career, reviewed it from time to time to remind me that being careful and alert can save an officer's life.

Let me go back to the chase; I have been at many auto accidents during my career, but I have never before or since seen anything quite like the one here. From the culvert on, debris was strewn along the highway for some fifty yards to where the car came to rest against the fence. The car had stayed upright, but the complete transmission sat in the middle of the highway, its gearshift sticking up. Gears, bearings, and pieces of the car's undercarriage littered the car's path on the highway.

When the fire department got the fire out, I noticed there was a double handful of tubes out of the radio in the front floorboards. I remember those old vacuum tubes were hard to remove from the radio, and required taking a firm grip and a determined pull to remove. I can only imagine what a shock must have gone through that car when it hit that abutment dead center at about 100 mph.

I would also like to say something about professional truck drivers. This was an isolated area. Other officers were scarce and backup was sometimes not available or, as in this case, miles and critical minutes away. By the time I got the people still at the scene out of their vehicle and secured in mine, truckers began stopping, directing traffic, cleaning debris off the highway and generally doing what needed doing. By the time the volunteer fire department and other help began to arrive, the scene was already under control thanks to professional truckers who helped me prevent what could have become a nightmare on the highway. This was not an isolated instance. I had assistance from professional truckers in many instances throughout my career.

Law enforcement is about ninety-five percent waiting, watching, patrolling, talking to informants, taking complaints, and other routine activities. The other five percent is heart-thumping, adrenaline-pumping activity and since I am writing this to entertain the reader, I will write of a few of the highlights of my career which extends twenty-six years beyond the time when I accepted the position as Deputy Sheriff of Knox County, Texas.

I will first say a few words about the cars I drove while I was a Deputy Sheriff. H.C. kept the car he was driving and I inherited the one Melton had been driving. It was a low mileage 1961 Ford 4 door sedan with full police package. The Ford had a 351 cubic inch engine, 15 inch wheels (14 inches was standard at that time), 3 speed manual transmission with a 30 percent overdrive, and the certified speedometer said it would go 120 mph on a flat road without too much wind interference.

When the Ford had been driven some 75,000 miles, it was beginning to be outdated as motors were getting more powerful and it would no longer overtake many cars on the road by that time. The Sheriff had gotten a 1964 Ford the year before. It had a 390 cubic inch motor and was a fine trip car as it would cruise easily at 80 to 90 mph, but was not as good a pursuit vehicle as it should have been because it arrived from the factory with a 3.50 to 1 rear axle ratio instead of the 4.11 it was supposed to have had. The Sheriff elected not to have it changed.

We discussed the situation and finally ordered a 1965 Plymouth with a 383 CID motor and automatic transmission. I don't remember the axle ratio but it was a good pursuit vehicle and would top out at about 125 mph. After about 2,000 miles, as it was just getting broken in, the piston rings wore the block enough to find a casting flaw in the block and a hole in the cylinder developed allowing cooling fluid into the cylinder. The car had to have a complete short block installed and the break in done again. I don't remember ever turning around on a vehicle that I didn't catch when driving this car, although I know there were some vehicles capable of better speeds. I wasn't involved in such a race, but I remember listening to one on the radio.

A Texas Highway Patrol unit out of Abilene turned around on a speeder near Abilene on Interstate 20 West and began pursuit toward Sweetwater some 50 miles distant. He called the Abilene dispatch and notified of the pursuit and asked dispatch to notify a Sweetwater unit to meet him. He was asked what kind of car he was pursuing and said it was a Corvette and that his speed was in excess of 120 miles per hour. There was a running conversation for the next few minutes with the patrolman giving his location regularly. From the way the officer was talking, I thought he was breathing fumes from the speeder's tailpipe and expected him to call a license number at any time.

Then he was asked how far the vehicle was ahead of him and he said, "About five miles." When I heard the trooper say he was five miles behind the Corvette, I just laughed and thought to myself, "That race is already over and the Trooper just doesn't know it yet." Of course, when he met the Sweetwater unit a few minutes later there was no Corvette between them, it having gotten out of sight of the pursuing Trooper and turned off, unseen, before encountering the Sweetwater unit.

I soon learned that the fastest car did not always win in a pursuit situation. After working a few months in Knox County, I knew all of the roads well, where the curves were, and how fast I could take them in my cruiser.

In one such case, I was just entering Knox City one night and met a car with no rear license plate. I turned around thinking that the vehicle might be stolen. When the driver saw my brake lights, he floored the accelerator and had a little lead in the beginning. My vehicle was equipped with a switch which would kill the brake lights on my vehicle to keep this from happening. I was negligent for not using it this time. The road had enough curves that although he gained a little on the straits, I more than made it up in the curves, and was right on his bumper as we approached Munday. I had called ahead by radio and the City policeman had set up a road block.

The runner could see red lights ahead, and tried to escape in a residential area. His luck was all bad that night as he left the highway and picked a dead end street. I plucked him out of a front yard at the end of the street. I met the city unit at the scene and gave the case to him after I found no stolen report and the driver's California license was valid. I remember him remarking as I took him out of my car, "That sure is a fast Ford." He never knew he had the faster vehicle. The vehicle he drove was a new Pontiac. He said he ran just because he did not think I could catch him. Although he did not have a rear tag, he was legal, and had a temporary sticker in the back window. I never knew just what the Munday policeman filed on him, but am sure he left town a wiser man than when he entered.

★ Chapter Three ★

Our new living quarters required major adjustments for both me and my wife, Sylvia. She had agreed to do food preparation for the prisoners and to keep from having to prepare extra meals, except in unusual circumstances, the prisoners ate the same food as did her family. This seemed the best arrangement because the average jail population was just a few (Usually from 3 to 6). This was during the time when the Bracero program was in effect, and there were some sizable barracks in the county in which to house the temporary workers. There were times during the summer months when we would have a crowded jail on Monday mornings until the prisoners could be taken before magistrates, pay fines, make bail, or otherwise have their cases disposed of.

When there was much more than normal jail population, she would usually make large pots of beef stew and pans of cornbread and beans or sandwiches for the prisoners. They were well-fed and no one ever lost weight while being confined in the Knox County jail while she was responsible for the prisoner's food.

The living quarters had a small office which contained a desk on which there was an extension phone from the phone in the office at the courthouse. There was also a radio and when the sheriff's office was closed I took all calls to the sheriff's office, no matter what the hour. This resulted in me being the first responder to many serious accidents and incidents.

Sylvia would almost always be awake when I had a call in the middle of the night and make any phone calls needed, such as to the wrecker service, Justice of the Peace, or other jurisdictions with which I did not have radio contact from my vehicle. The Sheriff had a radio at his home which he left on 24 hours and usually heard me if I called. I handled everything I could by myself and called him only in emergencies when I had to have assistance that way he would be fresh to open the office at eight o'clock in the morning and, if I had been up much the night before, I could sleep in until I was ready to get up and go to the office.

As I got settled into the Sheriff's Office and began to handle the paperwork, I noticed that much of the correspondence we received would be addressed to our office and signed for the sheriff of whatever county it was from by the Chief Deputy or in the case of Oklahoma and some other states, the Under Sheriff. Well, heck! I was Chief Deputy Sheriff of Knox County by virtue of being the only deputy in Knox County, and soon learned that our correspondence would receive a better response, particularly from larger departments, if I used the same format, which I continued to do for the time I was there. That is how I became Chief Deputy Sheriff.

Since I am writing from memory, I will have to be vague about dates but about two years after I was hired as deputy, the Sheriff got authority and budget to hire another deputy to work the Munday area and we became a three-man department. The Sheriff hired Doc Clark, a good, solid citizen in his fifties who, although he had no law enforcement experience, did have good judgment, knew the citizens in his area and was an invaluable asset to the department. I don't believe there was a single major case that Doc and I worked together that was not solved from the time he was hired until I left the department.

An example of a case Doc and I worked together was the burglary of a grocery in his area. The manager of the store went to work one morning and found the safe had been emptied of cash and the back door was unlocked. There was no sign of forced entry. Doc called and I went with him to investigate the crime. We found some prints on the safe, but none we could connect with the burglary. One of the store carts was found next to the entrance of the storeroom with several items of merchandise in it. The safe was not broken. It was a time-operated safe and had been set to open 30 minutes prior to opening of the store. This gave the employees time to get the money out of the safe and the cash registers ready for opening of business. Our investigation developed that in practice the manager and employees actually began arriving about 10 to 15 minutes before opening time.

We kept coming back to the items in the cart which had been left at the back near the entrance to the storeroom. I carefully dusted them for fingerprints and found a few partials, and some smudges on the cans, and bottles in the cart. All employees of the store said they routinely locked the back door before leaving for the day, but we could not find anyone who was absolutely certain that he had locked it that night. We could not find any prints in the bathroom which did not belong to employees. After we had gotten all the evidence we could at the scene, Doc and I put our heads together to look at the evidence.

It looked most likely that someone had pretended to be shopping, put a few items in a cart and waited until no one could see him, then went into the storeroom and hid until the store closed for the night. Since the safe had not been forced, we thought the burglar had waited until the timer went off and had taken the money from the safe during the time between when it opened and the time the employees arrived. This would have given only some 15 to 20 minutes and someone would have almost certainly been there to pick him up since Munday had a very active night watchman who would have found a strange car parked anywhere in the area. The pickup man would have to have known when to pick him up also. This convinced us that although it was possible someone had been lucky enough to find the back door unlocked, that would have been an almost unbelievable coincidence.

We decided it was almost certainly an inside job. We looked at the employees from the manager (who had been there less than a year) on down and found nothing. The cart with the items in it convinced us it was not left by an employee. We were at a dead end, and it was time to punt.

Most of our bigger crimes such as this one were committed by professional criminals out of one of the larger towns in the area. They operated on the idea that the rural areas had few officers and that they were smarter than any hick in the boondocks. What they did not know was, in the metropolitan area, there were few men assigned to burglary detail and there were so many offenses they often had less than 30 minutes to spend at any one scene, whereas we hicks in the boondocks had few offenses and could spend all the time it took to be thorough in such investigations. We were not necessarily as incompetent as they thought we were.

A little luck never hurt, and we had some in this case. The Sheriff had been kept up to date on our investigation and decided to talk to the Captain in charge of the burglary detail in the Police Department at Abilene. The Captain told H.C. that word on the street in Abilene was that two of their known burglars had made a big score somewhere and had been spending a lot of money recently. From what the Captain had told H.C. this looked like the timeline was about right. The money these guys were spending could have come from our burglary.

H.C. sent Doc and me to Abilene to see if we could make the connection. We took the fingerprints and also the items from the grocery cart with us and went to Abilene where we met with the Captain that H.C. had talked to on the phone. The Captain told us some of the background of the two men he and H.C. had talked about. The more he told us, the better our chances looked. I asked if their prints were on file and the captain had his fingerprint expert pull their files and compare their prints with what we had been able to obtain at our scene. The expert took my best partial print and after carefully checking both it and the next best one said, "This is your man, but I lack one identification point being able to make a positive ID from the witness stand in court."

I asked the Captain if he had done time in Huntsville and he said he had done time more than once. Most old cons are easier to talk to if they know you have the evidence than an amateur is. Many first timers will continue to lie even when you lay an airtight case out in front of them, whereas an old timer is often easy to talk to once he sees that he is caught. In this case, we knew we had the right man. I knew he would think his prints at the scene had led us to him and he would have no idea that we found him through his and his partners spending of the money. I asked the Captain if he could pick the man up for questioning or if he wanted a warrant first. He said the man would come in without a warrant. I asked him to have a detective bring the man in and I called the Sheriff in Benjamin, who got busy getting a warrant issued for the subject for burglary.

By the time the detective got the man to the office, we had a warrant number and were ready to go for broke. When they said he was waiting in an interrogation room, I asked the Captain to go in with us. We went into the room and Doc put the items from the grocery cart on the desk. These items were still discolored from the fingerprint powder. Then I told him I was from Knox County. He looked at the goods on the desk and then looked back at me and I could see him wilting like a weed in a Roundup commercial. There was not a doubt in his mind that the fingerprints on the items had led to our identifying him. He had not been very careful about prints on the items in the cart, because he did not think whoever investigated the burglary would ever connect the items to the burglary.

He was easy to talk to and the story he told was that he had gotten to know the previous manager of the grocery store (who had quit or been fired a few months prior) who had told him exactly how the job could be done and expected a share of the loot. He gave a statement giving his part in the job and that of the previous manager, but would not give up his companion, who I believed had picked him up as he left the store.

As for the previous manager of the store, he had disappeared sometime before the burglary was committed and left no forwarding address. A week or so later, I had occasion to be in Wichita Falls and went to the place where I had previously worked. There I was able to learn that the former manager of the store was in San Antonio, Texas, working for an auto dealership as a car salesman. I remember the Sheriff and County Attorney were planning a trip to the Austin area at that time and that they went on to San Antonio and handled the case from there on. I never saw him and, if I ever knew, I have forgotten if enough corroborative evidence was obtained to charge him in the case.

★ Chapter Four ★

Let's talk about the strangest, most controversial incident I dealt with during my tenure as Deputy Sheriff of Knox County. I have recounted this occasionally when I thought it appropriate and have had reactions from laughter at my ignorance to being told I was lying. Let me say right now that I am not trying to convince anyone of anything. I don't care one way or the other. This is what happened, the way it happened, and some of the people who witnessed it. I did not make a written report on it and do not know if anyone else did. I do not know the date or even remember the exact year. I know I was still driving the 1961 Ford, so it was prior to late 1964. I think it was 1963.

It was a warm evening shortly after dark when I left Benjamin. Nothing was happening and I was going to drive over to Munday and visit with Doc and see if anything new was happening in his part of the county. I had heard Ranger Melton check on duty headed for Seymour some ten minutes before I left Benjamin. I drove east on Highway 82 intending to turn south about seven miles out on Farm to Market Rd. 267 South and go through Rhineland, then on to Munday. I had just passed the little roadside park some four miles east of Benjamin on Highway 82 when I heard the radio operator in Seymour call Sheriff Wesley Styles and notify him that the gatekeeper on the Waggoner ranch had just called and reported that a strange aircraft had landed in the pasture by their house and he wanted someone to come and check it out.

The Waggoner ranch charged a trespass fee for access to Lake Kemp, which was a popular recreation area, and the access road was some seven miles north of Seymour. The gatekeeper was an employee who had lost a leg and collected the trespass fees. All vehicles had to pass by a booth built into the house in which he and his family lived. Sheriff Styles acknowledged the call and presumably started that way.

I continued east from the park on Highway 82. A couple of minutes after I passed the park, I saw an orange-colored light rise above the horizon ahead of me and slightly to my left. It traveled left to right and upward at about a 30 degree angle. The light was about half the size of a full moon and when it got to just about directly over the road in front of me, it just blinked out. The light was traveling fast, and was in sight only about two seconds. I knew Melton would be some ten miles ahead of me near the Red Springs community. I picked up the mike and asked him if he had seen that light. He replied that he had and that it was on ahead of him.

Just a minute or so later, the dispatcher at Seymour called the Sheriff again and told him that the gatekeeper had called again and said the aircraft they had called on had taken off and was now gone.

I believe it was reasonable to conclude at this point that the light we saw was the craft taking off from the Waggoner place. Given the fact that I was seven miles east of Benjamin and Seymour was 30 miles east of Benjamin, the craft was 23 miles east of me. I never knew if Sheriff Styles saw it or not. I do know of one other officer besides Melton and me who saw it.

The Foard County Deputy Sheriff happened to hear the traffic on the radio and was in the part of his county that adjoined Baylor County and was going down the road toward the gatekeeper's house when the craft left.

When I reached FM 267, instead of going on to Munday, I decided to just stop and listen to the radio and see if anything else happened. I stopped at the intersection of FM 267 and US 82 and parked next to the right-of-way fence on FM 267. I turned the volume up on the radio, left the door open, and sat on the hood of my car. It was a beautiful, clear night and traffic was light. I'm sure I paid more attention to the sky than usual since I had just seen something very unusual a short time earlier.

Fifteen to twenty minutes after parking I noticed two sets of lights in the sky. They were northeast of me and moving to the southwest from the Vernon area toward Abilene and passed just about directly over where the craft had been seen earlier. There were two sets of these lights and I have to believe they were attached to something. They moved together, one to the right and slightly ahead of the other. They were pretty high and passed over

Doc who was watching them from Munday after I had called his attention to them. I could hear no sound from them and Doc said he could not either. The reason I know they were high is that they became too distant to see when they were still at about a 45 degree angle in the sky.

These two were unlike the first one. There was a pulsating (not blinking) red light larger than the other lights on the vehicle. The other lights appeared to go all around the craft if the side I could not see was like the side visible to me. If the off side was like the side visible, then I can conclude that the vehicle was round or nearly so. The pulsating light would have been about the middle and the other lights which were red, orange, blue—white, green and perhaps another color that I do not remember appeared to rotate clockwise (when viewed from below) around the pulsating red light. By this time, I had gotten my binoculars out of the car, and was looking through them at the crafts.

I do not know if these perimeter lights were actually rotating around the craft or if they were in sequence. I believe I just forgot to notice as I should have been able to determine this. The blue-white light was like nothing I had ever seen and even though some of the new blue-white car lights we see now are similar, they still are not quite like the ones on this craft.

Some fifteen minutes after these two disappeared, another pair which appeared identical to the first (or perhaps the same two) appeared coming from the direction of Childress and going toward Waco. They passed over a short distance west of me. I had now seen these crafts from both sides and now knew they looked the same on one side as the other. By this time, I had Sylvia on the telephone checking with Sheppard AFB in Wichita Falls, Dyess in Abilene and Reece in Lubbock. They all said there were no military aircraft in our area.

Doc called me the following night about the same time and said he could see these lights again and that they were "changing colors on me." I talked to him the next time I saw him, but he had no new information. I did not know what these were at that time and I still do not know what they were. Here are just a few things I know they were not: stars, weather balloons, helicopters, conventional airplanes, lightning, swamp gas, mirages, reflections, the Aurora Borealis, or orbiting satellites, just to name a few.

★ Chapter Five ★

Since I mentioned the Waggoner ranch in the foregoing story, I'll say something about the area. The Waggoner Ranch was headquartered out of Vernon and comprised a sizable part of the northeast corner of Knox County, as well as much of several other counties in the area. It contained just shy of one half-million acres of land all under one fence. Although I never saw the field, I was told that one wheat field on the Waggoner was 10,000 acres. From there on west is what my friend Wyman Meinzer (more about him later) calls big ranch country, extending from there on west to the Llano Estacado and containing such well-known names as Pitchfork and Four Sixes, which was headquartered in Guthrie in King County adjoining Knox County to the west.

At that time, the Four Sixes still used cowboys and horses to do their roundups and also took an authentic chuck wagon into the pastures. Peace officers were welcome at any time and we would sometimes (when we knew where they were working) go to the chuck wagon and eat lunch with the cowboys. I believe I ate at least one breakfast there also as I remember sourdough biscuits, steak, eggs, and molasses at one meal.

The salt fork of the Brazos River entered the southwest corner of the county and exited about midway on the east side. North of the river were the ranches and the farming was mostly wheat and feedstuffs. South of the river was rich farm land, with potatoes being a big item in the Munday area where there was a cleaning and processing plant which shipped a lot of potatoes. There was also oil production in the county. I believe there were about 860 square miles in the county and, with some exceptions, was populated with honest, hard-working people. One of my favorite examples of the kind of people we had in the county can be illustrated by the following incident.

When my family began living in Knox County, my oldest

son, Steven, was ten years old, and one of his classmates was Wyman Meinzer, the son of Pate Meinzer, who managed a cattle ranch near Benjamin. I was in the Sheriff's office one day when I received a call from the Baylor County Sheriff's Department requesting a road block as they had just had an armed robbery and the involved vehicle containing four occupants had just been seen going west on Highway 82 toward Benjamin. I quickly drove to the intersection of Farm to Market Road 267 and set up a one man block as I was the only officer available at that time. Doc set up a block on Highway 277 in the Munday area.

I was expecting the suspected vehicle to pass in about 15 minutes when Pate Meinzer came by on his way home from Benjamin. He stopped to see what I was doing, and when I told him, he asked who was coming to help. I told him no one else was available. Without another word and without being asked, he pulled his pickup across the highway from mine, took his rifle from the rack behind the seat, laid it across the hood of the pickup, and called back across the road saying, "I probably can't keep them from killing you, but I'll bet I can make them wish they hadn't." I felt as safe with Pate backing me as I would have with any of the officers in the area, safer than with some of them. We held the two-man roadblock for some 15 minutes until the wanted vehicle was located east of Seymour going toward Ft. Worth. They had intentionally let themselves be seen going west, then doubled back to the east.

Our sons, Steven and Wyman, did not do so badly either. Steven retired from the U.S. Border Patrol where he was a supervisory officer and shortly thereafter took a position as the firearms editor of Texas Fish and Game Magazine, which he holds today. Wyman is a noted author of a number of books dealing with Texas and the native wildlife. He is also noted as a photographer and lecturer on the subject, as well as being the official photographer of the state of Texas. Steven and Wyman have maintained contact through the years and are still friends today.

As long as I am talking about Wyman, I may as well tell of an experience with him. When Wyman was 13 or 14 years old, he got a .243 Winchester caliber rifle that was very accurate, and he also got reloading equipment. I think he spent much of his spending money on powder, bullets, and related items. I was in Knox City shortly before I left Knox County. There was a shooting competition at the local gun club, and I saw Wyman there and asked if he had entered the competition. He said he did not have enough to pay the entry fee as he had already spent his money uptown. I don't remember asking him, but I was pretty sure the money had gone to shooting supplies. I knew he could shoot and thought he had a chance to win, so I paid his entry fee. I had to leave before he was due to shoot, but learned later that he had won the center fire competition against all comers.

I did not know it at the time I left, but there was a .22 caliber competition later in the day and another friend entered him. He won a turkey in that competition. All in all, it was a good day for the young 15-year-old. I spoke with Wyman recently and learned he had shot out three barrels. For you non-shooters, he wore out the first barrel, had it replaced two times, and wore out those barrels also, then had it re-barreled to .220 Swift and still has the rifle.

There were a couple of scalawags in the county who were not above a little tomfoolery when the opportunity presented itself. H.C. and I were working together one evening shortly after sundown when we stopped a vehicle coming away from a farm in an area where there had been some recent thefts. We did not recognize the car, so we stopped it to check for possible theft. It proved to be three young fellows who were working on the farm. They had a large barn owl in a sack. They had caught it someway in the loft at the barn. We talked to them a couple of minutes, then asked what they were going to do with the owl. They didn't have any plans and said they were going to turn it loose, away from the farm. The Sheriff and I looked at each other. He elbowed me in the ribs and asked if they would let us take the owl and turn him loose for them. They gave us the owl and we took it back to town.

The Chief of Police liked to read his paper every evening after dinner. He was in his office with his feet on his desk reading the paper. His car was parked on a side street at the side of city hall. The side street was not well-lit. I dumped the owl out of the sack and onto the front seat of the Chief's car. H.C. drove to a nearby alley where he parked the car. We had been careful not to let the chief know we were near town. H.C. then called the chief on the radio and told him we were coming to town and would buy his coffee if he wanted to meet us at the cafe. He got a 10-4 and we peeked around the building in the alley.

The Chief came out, opened the door of his car, and just sort of hopped in. He bounced right back out and the owl came out right behind him and flew off into the night. I can still see the Chief peeking into the car windows trying to see what had beaten him about the head and ears. We beat him to the cafe and were waiting for him when he arrived. We managed to both keep straight faces while we had coffee and talked shop for a while. We bought his coffee, though. He never said a word about the owl and we sure didn't. I don't know if he ever knew what was in his car or how suspicious he was as to how it got there. H.C. and I had a good laugh out of it anyway.

Bill Ryder operated a ranch in what we called the breaks north of Benjamin and located along the Little Wichita River. I considered Bill a rugged Texan who was not afraid of anything. He used horses to work the cattle on the ranch and rode animals which I did not even want to get in the corral with. I was at the ranch headquarters one day and Bill had just brought a sizable bobcat in. He and the cowboys had been working cattle and Bill had seen the cat, ran it down with his horse, roped it, and a fight ensued with the cat. After he found he could not escape the rope, he went on the attack. He jumped at Bill's legs and the horse's belly until Bill finally got the rope over a limb of a cedar tree and pulled the cat off the ground. He then tied a stick in his mouth, threw his coat over the cat and brought him to the house on his saddle. Bill tied the rope holding the cat to a tree in the yard and that was one "ticked off" cat. There were several young dogs around the place and while I was there, two or three of them discovered the cat and went to investigate. Any dog which came close enough for the cat reach got a lesson I'll bet he never forgot.

I was in the office at the courthouse one day shortly after I had gotten the 1965 Plymouth cruiser. Mrs. Ryder called on the phone and said that a child of one the employees of the ranch had fallen off a porch, hit his head, and was having some difficulty breathing. Bill asked her to call and ask if I would meet him on the highway at the entrance gate of the ranch and take him and the child to the hospital in Knox City some 16 miles distant. I agreed and arrived at the gate just as Bill's pickup stopped on the other side. He got out and helped the child's mother out of his pickup. She was holding the child who appeared to be some three years old. Bill put her in the back with the child and got in front with me and we set sail for the hospital.

As we went through Benjamin (one blinking red light—population about 350), I called and asked Knox City to alert the hospital emergency room and tell them we were bringing a child with a head injury and also to clear the traffic light that I would have to pass going through town. After we cleared Benjamin, I made a safe, but fast, run the remaining 12 miles or so to Knox City. When we went through the first curve out of Benjamin, Bill said that he thought the child was doing better. I told him I thought we had still better get him there as soon as possible and kept the speed up. I was busy driving and didn't notice until we stopped at the hospital, but, by this time, Bill was white as a sheet. There was not enough money in Texas to have gotten him back in that cruiser with me. I tried to persuade him to let me take him back to his vehicle, but he flatly refused. He called the ranch and had someone come to Knox City to pick him up.

I believe Bill told me every time we talked after that how scared he was during that ride. This was truly a matter of perspective. To Bill, it was a wild, hair-raising ride. To me, it was a routine fast ride to Knox City, the same as I would have made, and did make, routinely on any emergency call.

I'm sure it would have done Bill's heart good to have seen my face a few years later after I had gone to the Border Patrol and was riding as observer in a bell helicopter with Charlie "Ready" Rogers. Charlie was a fine pilot with a zillion hours of flying time. I liked to fly with him when the occasion arose. We had been up for an hour or so and were coming back to land at Uvalde. I think we were probably some twenty-five hundred feet above the airport at Uvalde when, without saying anything to me, Charlie did whatever pilots do to put the chopper into auto-rotation and we went into what felt like to me was freefall. Although I had never experienced auto-rotation before, I had heard of it, and before panic set in, I realized what Charlie had done, but for a few seconds, he had my undivided attention. He re-engaged the rotor and made a normal landing and we both had a good laugh at my initial reaction after we landed.

While I am thinking of reactions, this would be a good time to remember the time I got one from Sylvia. After I got my badge and handgun and learned what the price of practice ammunition was for the pistol, I soon bought some reloading equipment. By that time, I had made a friend in the person of the editor of the Knox City newspaper and had access to all the lead I needed. I would take my bullet mold to the offices of the newspaper and mold bullets until I had all I wanted, then go back to Benjamin and finish loading the practice ammunition. I had practiced with the pistol until I became quite proficient with it. I had hunted since I was 9 years old and was very familiar with guns, so it was not difficult to become proficient with the handgun.

On the day in question, I had been loading and had put primers in a few boxes of empty brass. I went to the kitchen to get something out of the refrigerator and noticed Sylvia was frying chicken for dinner and that dinner was almost ready. On an impulse, I put a brass shell with only the primer in it into the pistol and walked to the kitchen door just as Sylvia turned around from the stove with a platter of chicken in her hands. I said, "Sylvia, not chicken again? You know I don't like chicken!" Then I pointed the gun about 3 feet over her left shoulder and pulled the trigger. Being in the room, the primer made a loud pop and chicken went all the way to the ceiling and all over the floor. That was the evening I had chicken-a-la-floor for dinner. Not only did I eat it, I said it was good. Actually, it was no big deal as Sylvia kept her kitchen spotless and the tile floor was cleaner than many of the tables we find in the average café today. By the next day, she could smile about it and forgave me on the promise I would never do anything like that again.

★ Chapter Six ★

I was raised in rural south central Oklahoma and had hunted with shotguns and rifles all my life. When I was about nine years of age, I was allowed to begin hunting by myself in a wooded area near the house in which we lived on the farm. I was allowed to take only a single-shot shotgun. I hunted with this a couple of years until I was about 11 or 12 years old. I sold garden seed one year to win a prize. I sold enough seed to qualify and chose a brand new model BB rifle called the Red Ryder. I know this model is still being made today as I recently saw one in a local sporting goods store. I gave the sparrows around the house and barn fits with this gun and soon became proficient with this to the point that when going fishing, I just took the Red Ryder and an empty Prince Albert tobacco can along and shot grasshoppers for bait on the way to the creek.

I later graduated to hunting with my father's side-by-side 16 gauge double-barreled shotgun and became proficient with it also. I was also given a .22 caliber rifle and learned to use it to the detriment of many cottontail rabbits and squirrels which were abundant in the woods near the house. I even hunted to and from school sometimes. I could not take the .22 rifle onto the school grounds, but would hide it under a brush pile near the school and pick it up after classes. At that time, our house was about one-and-a-half miles from the school.

I told the foregoing to explain that I considered myself a pretty good shooter with several types of firearms when I took the job as deputy sheriff in Knox County. When the first dove hunting season arrived after we had moved to Benjamin, I was invited by a couple of local men to go hunting with them at the opening of the season. I had not had the opportunity to hunt for several years and was worried about being out of practice. I took my side-by-side double with me and accompanied the two fellows to a nearby field of maize where we found places to wait for doves. I believe they had a shot or two before my first opportunity arrived via a pair of doves coming right at my location. I took them both for a clean double and thought the four years of inactivity had hardly affected me as I was still a dead shot.

The birds continued to fly and I killed my next dove with my 18th shot. I had missed 15 straight shots and my self-confidence was in tatters as well as my reputation as a shooter. Before the day was over, I had downed a few more birds and was feeling somewhat better, but still not shooting as well as I knew I was capable of doing. The two men I hunted with that day were Claude Stockton and Lee Snailum. We became fast friends and hunted and fished together for the rest of the time I lived in Benjamin. I also hunted with the Sheriff. His wife owned a ranch of some eight thousand acres west of Knox City which had numerous coveys of quail and a number of ponds. The work at Benjamin required long, irregular hours and time off was limited, but, all in all, it was a good six years for me and my family.

I have talked about the good people of Knox County and they were abundant, but we had our share of not-so-desirable citizens also. Most of the population of the county was south of the Brazos river and most of the crime was also south of the river. Much of it was theft of oil field and irrigation equipment.

A typical case occurred one year when copper and brass became expensive. An irrigation supply company in Goree, Texas, in the southeast part of the county, was broken into and a considerable quantity of expensive brass valves, couplings, and other items were taken. The burglar had entered through a window in the building. No usable fingerprints could be found inside. Tracks of the burglar were very clear where he had jumped out of a window and landed in some oiled sand, which left a print almost as good as plaster of Paris. It was very distinctive in that the sole was composition rubber with stitching around the edge of the sole. On one side of the toe, the stitching had broken loose for an inch or so leaving a very distinctive mark.

I had been using a Polaroid camera in investigations even before moving to Knox county and continued to keep one in my car after being hired as a Deputy Sheriff. I took pictures of the footprints and laid a sheet of plywood over the tracks telling the people of the company to be careful not to disturb the area until further notice. I tracked the burglar across a vacant lot to where his vehicle had been parked on a gravel road and found nothing else useful. A description of the stolen items was given to offices in adjoining counties and they were asked to check with the salvage people in their respective areas. We soon found that items fitting the description had been sold at Haskell, Texas, in the adjoining county and that the people at the salvage yard could identify the person selling them if they saw him.

The Chief of Police in Munday knew one of his citizens was good for that kind of theft, and soon found an opportunity to look at his shoes. Bingo! The mark of the footprint at the scene of the burglary was a match. The Chief picked him up for questioning and called me. I went to Munday, took a picture of him, and talked a while to him. He was admitting nothing. I gave his picture to the Chief and he took it to the salvage yard in Haskell, and I took the subject to Goree and let him watch me place his shoe by the track in the sand by the Irrigation Company and take a picture of it. It was a perfect match.

By the time I got back to Munday, Doc had gotten a warrant and the people in Haskell had made positive identification of the man as having sold the stolen goods. When this man went to court, his lawyer pled him guilty and asked for probation which was granted by the district judge. I did not believe he deserved probation, but my opinion did not mean much to the court and the District Attorney did not object. After the proceeding, I told the defendant that I did not believe he would meet the terms of his probation and if and when I caught him again I would personally deliver him to the Walls (the admission facility of the Department of Corrections in Huntsville, Texas).

A few months later, winter arrived and there were patches of snow on the ground when we received word that a theft had occurred on a farm southwest of Knox City. Doc met me at the farm and we began the investigation. The ground was damp from melted snow. The theft was of copper radiators and batteries from tractors and other farm equipment. Tools were also taken.

Look as we might, we could find no tracks around the house, barns, or across the yard that could not be accounted for. We started looking farther afield and located where a car had pulled into a field, and backed out leaving the way it had come in. There had been no other car even near the farm place since the snow. We were scratching our heads until I noticed a trail of barely visible scuff marks leading from where the car had turned around up to the house and barn area a distance of some one hundred yards. Suddenly, I knew who had done the job and how he had done it.

The case was solved, now all I had to do was prove it. My old friend from the irrigation equipment job had struck again. He had seen me make a case against him by his tracks and he was not letting that happen again. He had tied burlap sacks around his feet and was not leaving tracks at this scene. What he did not know from the last case was that I had also tracked him to his vehicle the last time. I got my camera and began taking pictures of the tire prints that he had left when he turned around. They were as distinctive as his shoes had been in the last case. Every tire had a different tread, different amount of wear and some even had distinctive marks on the sidewalls. It was easy to tell which tire was on which wheel as he had pulled into the field going forward and backed out to turn around. I was also able to find a place where I could get a photograph of the pattern of the burlap he had tied around his shoes. It took us a couple of days to locate him and his car. We found him in the Haskell county jail and his car impounded there. We drove to Haskell to take pictures of his tires and as expected found a perfect match. The burlap sacks were still in the trunk of the car.

The Sheriff in Haskell had been having the same kinds of thefts in the north part of his county and, after seeing what we had on our case, solved a number of cases in his county against this same fellow. I not only kept my promise to this guy, I arranged for my parents to take care of the children, and feed the prisoners a couple of days and took Sylvia with me to Huntsville for a well--deserved overnight trip.

I can remember catching only one burglar actually in the building and in the process of burglarizing the place. I was in

Munday one evening, working with Doc Clark. The Sheriff was also in that area in his vehicle. The Chief of Police of Munday called on the radio and said that someone had just called him and reported they had seen someone in one of the local clothing stores moving about with a flashlight. The Chief had called the owner of the store and no one was supposed to be in the store. Doc and I went to the back of the store and the Sheriff and Chief of Police went to the front and waited for the owner to bring keys. We all kept out of sight until the owner arrived with keys then moved into position and the Sheriff and Chief went into the building at the front. Doc was at the back door. I had climbed a nearby ladder to cover the roofs as we did not yet know where or how entry had been made. We also did not know how many people were in the building, but by this time we had it covered.

As the officers in front were searching the building, the back door popped open and a man almost ran over Doc as he tried to escape. Doc grabbed him by the back of his belt, and the man was so intent on running that he just kept running, but was not making any progress as the old cowboy had dug in his heels and was holding him like he would a roped steer. I had come off the ladder and was going to help Doc, but before I got there, Doc had enough of his shenanigans and I heard him say, "OK, you son of a bitch, you want to run, let's see if you can outrun this." He pulled his revolver and turned the guy loose. The man said, "No, sir, I don't believe I want to."

I don't know if Doc would have actually have shot him or not but I would have done just what the burglar did if I had been in his place.

★ Chapter Seven ★

As I settled into my work at Benjamin, I began to realize that I had been extremely fortunate in my choice of positions. H.C. Stone proved to be the employer that every employee dreams of finding. His position as sheriff was an elective office and he had been appointed to fill the balance of Melton's term, I think there were about 3 years remaining. H.C.'s idea of running for re-election was to just be the best sheriff possible. He might do a favor here and there, but only if it did not interfere with honest, fair law enforcement in the county. I learned this early on when someone jokingly told me I could not do something as to do so might offend one of the county commissioners. H.C. had overheard the remark and promptly set the fellow straight. He told the man I was under no restrictions, and if I found anyone in the county, including a commissioner, in violation to the point of need to be arrested, I would be expected to do so and would have his full support.

I worked with him, rather than for him, and during the six years we worked together, we never had a serious disagreement and I was never directed to do anything unethical. He also did a full share of the field work. I have mentioned some cases that I worked with Doc (and we made some good ones), but in the meantime, H.C. was making his share and using his sources of information to help with any case I might be working on at the time.

Just to give an overview of how Sheriff Stone felt about the law enforcement people in general, I can remember an incident in which we had a burglary of the post office in the little town of Truscott, which was in the northern part of the county. The building had been broken into and the safe was hauled outside of the town where it was broken open and the contents taken. This burglary appeared to be a professional job as we found very little evidence and were unable to identify the burglars. The cash was taken, as well as the money orders. Several months later, we got a call from the Harrah's casino in Reno, Nevada. Two men were gambling in the casino and were cashing money orders bearing the stamp, or seal, from the Truscott post office. The casino was suspicious.

They were the ones stolen in Truscott, and the men were arrested and detained. The extradition papers were prepared and Stone and Bullington, the county attorney, went to Reno to bring them back. As they were coming back with the prisoners and driving down Interstate 40 in Arizona in the 1964 Ford I have previously said was a good trip car, they were red-lighted by a young Arizona highway patrolman. Stone was driving, and the young patrolman, who stopped them was indignant at the speed Stone was driving, asked, "Sheriff, what would you do if I came driving through your county like that?" Without hesitation, the Sheriff replied, "Son, if you had time to stop, I would buy you a cup of coffee. If you had prisoners and were in a hurry, I would give you a red-light escort from county line to county line." This account was given by Bullington after they returned to Benjamin. I worked six years with the man, and I can assure that Stone was telling the young patrolman the simple truth.

One of the cases the Sheriff and I worked on was the burglary of a hardware and gun store in Knox City. Among the items stolen were 15 or so guns, including a few pistols and an assortment of both new and used rifles and shotguns. I never knew the details of his investigation, but I know he worked on this for quite some time. He developed information that he was getting so close to the thieves that they became scared and threw the guns into a pond on some ranch west of Knox City. He had trouble learning which pond, but he was able to narrow it down to two possibilities.

We borrowed two strong magnets from the sheriff's department in King County and found two small aluminum boats. We tied rope to the magnets and dragged the first pond without finding anything, but we had better luck on the second one. The magnets were strong enough to pull the guns up out of the mud. It was a lot like fishing. The boat would be moving slowly through the water, and when the magnet got close to a gun, it would pull it up. The gun hitting the magnet would feel much like a fish hitting a lure. We had a car trunk full of wet, muddy guns when we finally quit dragging. As I said at the beginning, this was the Sheriff's case.

I no longer remember what disposition was made of this case. What I do remember is that the insurance company had already settled with the store owner and wanted nothing to do with a bunch of waterlogged guns. The store owner had no use for them and we were able to buy any of the guns we wanted for a few dollars each. I bought several (I think four) of the guns, removed the wood, and persuaded Sylvia to put them in her oven and leave them at just enough heat to get rid of the moisture in the wood. I managed to salvage the guns, making them usable again. It required a lot of work as the wood had to be completely refinished and the metal had to be cleaned, polished, and re-blued, but, in the end, I came out with several usable guns, one of which had a factory-installed, adjustable choke, with which I later hunted.

The children were growing and doing well. Steven was reaching his teens and roamed the countryside with his school friends and his younger brother, David, who was four years younger. They hunted and explored, and they were growing up in the way I had always hoped they would. I bought Steven a rifle and he learned to call predators using a Weems predator call. A friend with whom I hunted showed him a call made from a tip of a goat's horn and he and his friends learned to make their own calls. I had trouble keeping any tool which had a plastic handle as it was likely to end up as a tool without a handle, and the plastic handle end up as a predator call. The city-owned lake was close enough to reach by bicycle and the boys spent a lot of time around the lake. Sylvia and I were both busy but, overall, we were happy and our family was doing very well.

★ Chapter Eight ★

Not every case ended the way we would have liked. We had an appliance store in Knox City which reported that they received a bad check for two television sets. The investigation uncovered that the man wrote the check from the Knox City Bank. The man told the appliance dealer that he was buying the motel in Benjamin, that two of the televisions were not working at all, and he intended to replace them all soon. The dealer, seeing a big sale ahead, did not question him closely, resulting in his getting stuck with a bad check. When we spoke to the bank, we discovered the forger had made a $5,000 deposit by writing a check for that amount on a bank in Carrizozo, New Mexico. The Knox City Bank had accepted the deposit subject to collection and given a deposit slip so stating. The New Mexico bank deposit had been from a bank in Pueblo, Colorado, and so forth.

The Sheriff gave me the case and told me to find the fellow, if possible. By that time, I knew it was going to take some in-depth investigation and probably a lot of phone calls. I asked about the cost and was told to work on it until he told me to stop. No limit.

I spent the better part of a day making long distance phone calls and learned that the car he was driving was a Mercury which he had bought in Oregon, also with a fraudulent check. I got the license number from the dealer in Oregon who had sold him the car. I finally got his correct name from the dealer who saw his driver's license. This man was a paper hanger and had a long offense record with jail time included. I notified all of the people I contacted that we wanted him, would extradite if he was found, and requested that we be informed if he was heard from.

We now knew who he was, but he had no permanent address and no way of knowing where he was. After several days, we received a call from the Knox City Bank that reported they were on the phone with a bank in Tennessee who claimed the man was in their bank, attempting to make a transfer deposit from the Knox City Bank. He had somehow made them suspicious, thus the call. The Sheriff told our bank to ask the Tennessee bank to stall him, and we would have the Sheriff there shortly. The bank in Tennessee did as we requested and managed to keep the subject waiting until the Sheriff or a deputy arrived and arrested him. It was a close call, though, as he had gotten suspicious and was leaving as the officer arrived.

Well, we had our man, and I sure felt good about it. We were busy getting the extradition papers ready as he had told the people in Tennessee he would not waive extradition. We called Tennessee and learned that the wily old con had asked to talk to an FBI agent. He confessed to the FBI that he had stolen the Mercury car in Oregon by a fraudulent check and offered to plead guilty to a Dyer Act Violation (interstate transportation of a stolen motor vehicle). The FBI agent obviously took the attitude of: "To hell with those people in Texas, I've got a bird's nest on the ground here and I'm going to take it." The Sheriff in Tennessee went along, and by the time we learned about it, he had already released the subject and he was in federal custody. There was nothing we could do except send a detainer and hope it got transferred whenever the man was moved. That was still pending when I left Knox County. The old con probably spent a few months in a cushy federal facility and was released.

We may have gotten even (or partially so) a few months later when we apprehended a couple of men from the same general area of Tennessee driving a stolen Volkswagen. We called the Sheriff of the county where they stole the vehicle and held them until the people from Tennessee came for them. The next time the FBI agent who worked our area came by our office, we told him about the case and told him to give the agent in Tennessee our regards. I never heard if he did or not. I do know this, though: the agent in Tennessee did not do his agency any favors as I never forgot the arrogant way he handled himself in this matter and neither did Sheriff Stone.

I would be willing to wager that almost everyone has known someone to whom trouble just seems to gravitate. They may have been likable and for the most part pretty good people, but were in some kind of difficulty almost every time you saw them. There were two such people in Knox County who lived in the same community. One was a woman, the other a man. One night they got into an argument which quickly escalated into a full scale fight. She took a swipe at him with a knife or razor and missed his throat by very little, but did take about half an inch off the lobe of one of his ears. He, in turn, emptied a nine millimeter automatic pistol at her without doing any damage, except to the neighbors' houses. Both wound up in jail.

The District Attorney was not interested in any felony charges, so the County Attorney filed on both of them for aggravated assault in county court. When the cases went to court, the judge gave each a fine and also gave the man thirty days to serve in the county jail. As I was processing him for entry into the jail, he complained that he received a stiffer sentence than had the woman. I pointed out that he had endangered the entire community, while she had not and suggested that possibly the fine was for shooting at her and the thirty days was for missing her. I asked how he could miss if she was close enough to take his ear off with a knife. He said that he forgot that the gun did not have a cartridge in the chamber and there had been a snap the first time he pulled the trigger. He further said that by the time he had worked the slide and chambered a cartridge, she was a moving target. I'll bet she was at that point.

Although the Sheriff was in charge of the jail and was responsible for its operation, my wife, Sylvia, had a lot more to do with its operation than either of us. She cooked the meals for the prisoners and fed them. She also answered the office phone when both the Sheriff and I were out of the office, which was often. This was in the early 1960's and segregation was still in effect. Regardless of this, Sheriff had an equal opportunity department. Our black, Latino and Anglo citizens were treated equally. The jail was the same, and, as far as Sylvia and I were concerned, the jail was also integrated. We occasionally had male trustees do maintenance work on the jail and grounds and on public facilities in other parts of the county, such as the city-county hospital in Knox City.

On rare occasions, a female would be allowed trustee status

to help Sylvia with upkeep or cleaning inside the jail office or living quarters. When this occurred and the female trustee was in the living area at meal time, Sylvia set her a place at the table and she ate with the family. This created quite a stir in the black community and I noticed that some of the black women were uncomfortable when I happened to be there at meal time and sat at the table with them. One such woman and Sylvia became close friends and corresponded back and forth by letter after we left Benjamin and moved to South Texas. She was a young, single mother to a couple of small children. She had served out a fine and 3-day jail term for DUI. When she was discharged from jail, Sylvia filled a big sack with clothes that our boys had outgrown and other items she could use. She was basically a fine person who had made a mistake and never made another while we were there, although she did maintain contact with Sylvia, and valued her advice which she sought from time to time.

During the six years we were at the jail, we never had an escape. We did have one trustee abscond. He was being held on the minor charge of stealing a license plate from one vehicle and using it on another. He was picked up by another agency a few days later and charged with a felony in that jurisdiction. We never even went after him or placed a detainer. The only serious attempt at escape came from three till tappers from the Los Angeles area. They were typical of the people I talked about earlier who considered that the rural area had only incompetent hicks who were much too slow to compete with them. They had hit a grocery store in Knox City, had been a little too slow on the getaway, and found themselves residents of the Knox County Inn while awaiting indictment for felony theft.

For those not familiar with this operation: till tappers usually operate in teams of two or three. They find a check-out counter with a cashier they believe they can distract. One of them gets a couple of items and go to the clerk, put his items on the counter, and gives the clerk money. As soon as the clerk opens the cash register, he decides he wants another item, one which is to one side of the register, usually at the bottom of a display case. As soon as the clerk squats down to get his item, his partner reaches across the counter and rifles the till, taking the large bills and often the cash sack which is usually under the cash tray. If the partner is not quite finished rifling the cash, he will find something else he wants until his partner has gotten the cash and restored the tray so that it looks normal. If it goes as planned, they have the cash and are out the door and gone before the theft is discovered.

Somehow, possibly a trustee told them or they overheard two trustees say something about my leaving, but they had discovered I was gone. They used some soap to get a quantity of foam and then one of them put it on his face and around his mouth. They raised a cry and a trustee notified Sylvia that something was wrong. They were saying one of them was having a seizure. Sylvia checked the cell block and they tried to get her to open the door. They were trying to fool an expert on soap suds with soap suds. Sylvia didn't buy it for a minute and made fun of him, asking how the soap tasted. She then called the sheriff who was nearby and he handled it from there. Even if the man had been having a seizure, she would have not opened the cell block. She had been thoroughly briefed about this possibility and thus ended the great jail break attempt.

I believe the most belligerent, confrontational, and unrepentant prisoner we had in the jail during the time I was there was a member of the Latin community. She was originally from Mexico and was as close to an authentic bruja ("witch") as I have ever encountered, even after twenty years in the U. S. Border Patrol. We were told she claimed the power of the Mal Ojo ("evil eye") and also claimed to be a curandera, which means a healer or healing woman. She reportedly claimed the ability to heal various ailments, including female problems, and victimized the ones who believed her.

The constable serving the community in which she lived told me of a man in her community who she told she was going to put the evil eye on unless he paid her a certain sum of money. He refused and she let it be known he was under the spell. It preyed on his mind until he developed a stomach ulcer or ulcer-like symptoms which grew worse until he relented and paid her. At the time, this fellow reportedly lived across the county line in Baylor County while I was working on another complaint. He never complained to us and considering how afraid of her he was reported to be, I doubt that he ever complained in Baylor County either. In any event, it never came to our attention officially.

A young woman went to H.C., complaining that the woman was trying to extort money from her by either blackmail or a threat. I remember staking out the drop area (the place the woman was to leave the money) and spending one long night waiting for her to pick up the money. The stake-out failed and I never knew the reason. H.C. was finally able to make a "practicing medicine without a license" case and arrested her. When the Sheriff opened the cell door, instead of entering, she began to fight. She tried to choke him by grabbing his necktie, but as John Wayne would say "he weren't no pilgrim." That move had been tried before and he now wore the clip-on style tie. I took the tie away and together we were able to put her in the cell without injuring her.

The next morning when Sylvia fed the prisoners, she called me to come and I found that this woman had torn all her bedding up and flushed it down the commode. The entire floor of the jail was almost ankle deep in water as she kept running the water after stopping up the commode. It took the trustees a full day to clean up the jail floor and a plumbing crew the better part of two days to get everything unstopped. Benjamin did not have a city sewer system and septic systems were used. We had everything back in order and she was now sleeping on the bare metal bunk.

The next morning, we found the water on the floor again and the commode stopped up. She had used every stitch of her clothing except a pair of pedal pusher-type slacks, including her shoes and socks, and stopped things up again. Back came the plumbers and the trustees got out the squeegee and mops again. All privileges were suspended and nothing was allowed in the cell that would stop up a commode. It probably took a week before she was willing to agree to behave in a civilized manner in exchange for bedding and clothing. She agreed to this only after she realized it was harder on her than it was on us and that she could not cause enough trouble to make us release her.

She had some fetish concerning blonde hair and tried repeatedly to entice my daughter, Lisa, close enough to her cell so she could touch her blonde hair. Lisa was born after we came to Benjamin and was four years old at this time. I have since come to believe this fetish had to do with warding off the evil eye or conferring it. I have also heard that it is just to bring good luck. Whatever the reason, Lisa was terrified of her.

Shortly before we left Benjamin, my wife's brother was hired as the boys' athletics coach by the high school and we continued to go back to visit his family and I continued to see H.C. from time to time after we moved away. One of the last times I saw him, he still was not doing the FBI any favors because of the shafting we got by the FBI agent in Tennessee. He chuckled and said that an agent was trying to get his fingerprints. I asked why in the world an FBI agent would want his prints, and he said there had been a fire at the curandera's place and the agent thought he had found pieces of glass from a Molotov cocktail at the location and that, apparently, one piece of the glass had a print on it, or at least a partial print. The Sheriff continually had so much trouble from this woman that he did not much care what trouble she had and hoped it would cause her to go elsewhere. Since he would not cooperate with him in the case, the FBI agent thought that he might have something to do with the fire.

The Sheriff was having a fine time playing hide-and-seek with the agent. Knowing H.C., I would make a serious bet that he never threw a Molotov cocktail at anyone, but I wouldn't bet a plugged nickel that he did not have a darned good idea who did if, in fact, one had been thrown in the first place. I didn't ask him if he thought there was actually arson or how the FBI became interested in the first place.

★ Chapter Nine ★

We were involved in manhunts an average of three or four times a year. By manhunt, I mean the kind where a fugitive is known to be in a certain area but has gone to ground. This usually occurs after an armed robbery or a homicide or some other offence, such as when a stolen car is being pursued and the thief abandons the vehicle and runs. Since Knox County and the adjoining counties are mostly rural and sparsely populated, this often results in all of the roads around the area where the suspect or suspects were seen being blocked and everything that moves being checked in order to contain the fugitives in the smallest area possible until they are found and apprehended. Since there were so few officers in each jurisdiction, this resulted in officers coming from all directions to help. Some were resolved right away and others took considerable time. Let's look at one of each, beginning with the long one.

We learned by radio that some sort of assault involving a gun had occurred in a rural area near Dickens, 60 miles west of Benjamin. A suspect had been pursued, abandoned a vehicle, and gone to ground in a rural area northwest of Guthrie. This was just after dark. Deputy H.C. and I went in our individual units, prepared to help in any capacity necessary. We arrived, as did units from other jurisdictions, and we soon had all roads blocked far enough away from the abandoned vehicle to insure that the fugitive was within the circle. Other officers searched likely areas and notified area citizens to take precautions, be on the lookout, and to report any sighting. Being the mid-1960's, we did not have handy-talkies, cell phones, helicopters, or planes. We held the roadblocks and continued to work through the night and the next day, without success. The roadblocks were moved back and held through the next night and the next—still no sign of the fugitive.

While the Sheriff and I were doing this, Doc was driving to Benjamin each day and keeping our department operating. Finally, on the morning after the third night, Doc called and notified us that he had the subject in custody. A Knox County resident who lived a few miles west of Benjamin had spotted the man near his house, called our office, and Doc had arrested the man without incident. The man had disposed of the gun and, to my knowledge, it was never found. Upon questioning, we learned this man had walked at night and hid during the days. He had walked north close enough to Paducah to see the town lights, but had been scared off by a road block and turned east, continuing to walk until he was apprehended. The best we could estimate, he had walked just short of 70 miles. Most of us hadn't had our boots off since the manhunt started and all of us were exhausted.

Now, let's look at an easier manhunt. The Sheriff's Department in Seymour, Baylor County was involved in a chase of a vehicle which had been stolen earlier in the day in the Ft. Worth area. The two men in the car abandoned it at the edge of town, ran down a street, and were lost nearby. Again, we went to help and were on the scene in less than an hour. Using my flashlight, I found two sets of barefoot tracks leading into a cotton field at the end of the street where they were lost. Shoes in the vehicle convinced us that the barefoot tracks were our men, but I could not move them any further. We held a perimeter all the rest of the night and I intended to resume tracking as soon as it got light enough to see the tracks.

The cotton in the field was waist high and had bolls which were nearly mature. Sheriff Styles had driven his car close to where I was waiting. Just as it was getting light enough to see, those of us around the field saw two heads come up for a look from about the middle of the field. They quickly ducked back down, but we had a line on them. I started walking that way, but Sheriff Styles was already in his car. He aimed his car directly at the place where he saw the heads and opened it up. He was about 150 yards from where the men were. By the time the sheriff got halfway there, he was driving 40 miles per hour and cotton bolls, leaves, and other debris were going ten feet in the air over his car. It made the darndest racket you ever heard and scared the fugitives half to death. They were jumping up and down and waving their hands in the air. By this time, they were hoping they would live long enough to surrender and trying to attract the sheriff's attention so they wouldn't go the way of the cotton field. That ended our part in this manhunt. It cost us a night of sleep, but it was well worth it to see those city boys come to attention when the sheriff's car started harvesting that cotton field.

I have been telling how I worked my fingers to the bone solving difficult cases right and left, but the truth is that not all cases were that difficult. Technology was not nearly as sophisticated as it is today. Our assigned radio frequency was 37.180 MHz and "skip" was common. Sometimes, we would hear radio traffic from thousands of miles away so strong that it would be difficult to communicate with our own units just a few miles away. I was sitting in our office one day, minding my own business, when I heard the Sheriff in Haskell say something about a car that was going to have the gas tank cleaned out because it had so many coins in it that it would hardly run. I believe he had formerly been a mechanic and could have just been talking about a car in a friend's garage.

I remember hearing a police department in, I think, Wheeler or Shamrock, Texas, a while earlier talking about a home burglary where a coin collection worth big bucks was taken. This was some of the skip traffic I mentioned above as this town where the coins were stolen was much further than we could usually communicate. I radioed Sheriff Garth in Haskell and asked what he had on the occupants of the car in question. He said that he didn't have much, but he thought they would be good for about anything. I told him what I had heard earlier and suggested he contact this department and see if he did not have the coin collection they had lost in the gas tank of his car. Yep! It was a match! A good solid case was made on a home burglary and I didn't even have to do the paper work. My total elapsed time was about five minutes.

I would be willing to bet that most of my readers have witnessed from one to several law enforcement units parked at a coffee shop, doughnut house, or other cafe and thought that the officers inside should be out working instead of sitting inside and increasing their belt size and getting even more lazy. I'm not going to say you are always wrong. I will say, however, that some of my best cases both as a Deputy Sheriff, and later as a U. S. Border Patrol Agent, came about as a result of information received in just such a manner. Even if all the cars are from the same department, they are almost surely talking shop unless the waitresses are all Miss America contestants. If there is more than one department represented they are talking shop and exchanging information, even if the waitresses do all look like Miss America. I remember one such gathering where one officer was telling us about a loss of handy-talkies and another officer from another jurisdiction, sitting at the same table, admitting with a red face that he had bought the same handy-talkies just a few days prior for his department. I don't know how the stolen report got overlooked, but I do know it got straightened out at that table over a cup of coffee. I know there are some guys who can goof off with the courthouse on fire and the bank full of robbers, but that is not the norm.

Radar was being used by the Texas Highway Patrol officers in the mid-1960's, but it was much more primitive than the sophisticated units we see on the highways today. Highway 82 through our area had one of the highest average speeds of any highway in the state. The way it was done at that time required two units or usually three officers or more. The radar unit was mounted on a tripod and set at the side of the pavement. One officer sat in a car parked next to the radar unit and read the recorded speeds on a dial inside his car. He then radioed the speed of any violator to a catch unit stationed one-half mile ahead. The radar unit registered speeds up to 100 mph and it was not at all unusual to hear the man reading the speeds call out that his dial had been pegged by the "next car to you." The lights would be activated by the catch unit and the violator watched until he was stopped. It was not unusual for a violator to see the radar as he passed it and to stop, or turn around and run to avoid the consequences of being caught. Although we of the sheriff's department were not traffic officers, we often had a unit (usually me) waiting with the catch car. If a DWI or other person requiring a full custody arrest, instead of the usual traffic ticket, was arrested, I could accept custody on the spot and transport the arrested person to the jail, leaving the full radar crew to continue their work.

It was during such an operation that one of the most tragic incidents of my tenure at Benjamin occurred. I was working with the catch units one night when the Sheriff's Department at Guthrie, twenty-five miles west of where we were working, called by radio and informed us that they had a report that a man had left a place of business there who was intoxicated and was driving a 1959 Chevrolet car coming our way. I told the guys at the check point I would go to meet this car and see if I could possibly get him off the road before he killed someone.

I was three miles west of the point when I met a car I thought might be it, but as we passed I could see that instead of the large horizontal tail lights of a '59 Chevrolet, the car had the smaller round lights of a 1960 or '61 model. I met him on the crest of a hill and he was in sight for only a few seconds. He was on his side of the road and looked okay. I continued west looking for the 1959 model for about 2 more miles until the people at the point called me to say they had a head-on just west of the check point.

When I got back there, the scene was under control and I found that a young college student from the Ft. Worth area was already deceased in the westbound car. The eastbound car contained a drunk sitting behind the steering wheel of the 1960 Chevrolet I had met on the hill and he did not have a scratch on him. He had veered into the westbound lane and collided with the car driven by the student. I do not know whether I could have turned around, caught him and got him stopped before he met the student or not, but I would at least have had a chance if the person in Guthrie had just known the difference between a 1959 and 1960 Chevrolet.

To this day, that incident leaves a bad taste in my mouth when I remember it. The drunk was jailed in Knox County and charged. His girlfriend from the Lubbock area came a day or two later and made bond for him. I don't remember his being tried and believe his case was pending when I left Knox County.

From time to time we would have a violent death from something other than a car accident, but most of them had not, so far, presented any mystery. Believing that it pays to be prepared,

I made arrangements to attend when the Texas Department of Public Safety scheduled a week long seminar dealing with homicide investigations. This was held in Austin, and featured the Harris County coroner and experts in various other areas of homicide investigation. The coroner was a leader in his field, and presented a considerable number of film presentations dealing with various kinds of cases and causes of death. All in all, this was an interesting and informative seminar and I learned a lot.

The knowledge I gained from the film and lectures of the coroner helped in the resolution of a capital murder case which I will discuss later in this book. I also had opportunity to meet officers from all over the state and even out of state, as two attendees were deputies from the Sheriff's Department in Baton Rouge, Louisiana. It was a pleasure to talk shop with those guys.

The seminar ended shortly after noon on Friday and I decided to drive home that afternoon rather than spend another night in Austin. As I was arriving in radio range of Knox County, I could hear radio traffic indicating the sheriff was working a stabbing incident in Knox City and that the victim had just been declared dead on arrival at the hospital. I thought this might be an opportunity to use my newly-acquired expertise in homicide investigations, but by the time I arrived in Knox City, the case was already wrapped up.

A woman was being roughed up by her boyfriend and her 15 year old son had come to her defense. He had stabbed the deceased with his pocket knife and it was bye-bye boyfriend. The interesting thing about this case was that the kid had stabbed the man with the little blade of the knife. The blade, although sharp, was only one- and-a-half inches long. The boy had stabbed the victim in the chest and the blade had penetrated just enough to nick one of the arteries where it joined the heart. By the time anyone realized the wound was serious, the victim had almost bled out and was deceased before he reached the hospital.

This incident reinforced a decision that I had already made and which remained throughout my law enforcement career: anyone who pulled a knife on me had just introduced a knife into a gun fight. I had no intention of being carved up while trying to subdue anyone who was armed with a knife.

During the latter part of my tenure in Knox County, the game warden responsible for enforcement of the laws pertaining to fish and wildlife was named Vic Lowery. He was stationed in Knox City. I am not sure of the boundaries of his area of responsibility, but do know that Haskell County was part of his area. Vic was a hard-working officer and I liked to work with him. He was also a first class investigator. I was not actively involved, but knew of a case which he worked. A quail hunting lease on a local ranch was leased to a group of people from, I believe, the Dallas-Fort Worth area. One year Vic caught a hunter leaving the ranch in possession of many more birds than allowed by the law. Vic filed the applicable case against the violator, but he apparently considered the game limits a minor inconvenience not pertaining to him. Vic showed me a statement indicating the ranch manager and his wife had both killed limits of birds and given to the hunter. Vic said some other hunters on lease had either filed affidavits or given statements that they had also killed limits of birds and given them to the defendant.

The County Attorney became involved when Vic needed some time before the case went to trial. I never knew all the details, but do remember that before Vic was through with the case, he was prepared to prove the manager's wife did not have a license and the hunter in question was begging Vic to just let him plead to the original charge. Vic had gone to the Dallas-Ft. Worth area and found proof that some of the other affiants working at the time said they were hunting and could not have given the hunter any birds. I never knew (or don't remember) just how the case was resolved, but do know that word soon got around that a person had better get his ducks all in a row before he started messing around with Vic.

One year Vic came to me with a problem. It was shortly after dove season had opened that year. Vic had been in Haskell County a day or two prior and had filed on one or more hunters on a particular lease there. I believe they had been driving around the maize fields and shooting doves from the back of their pickup. Apparently, one of the hunters on that lease was a very important person or considered himself a tough guy. He had apparently gone with the hunter to the Haskell County courthouse to pay the fine and let it be known that he wanted that game warden to know that he intended to hunt his doves any way he wanted to and that it would not be a good idea for any warden to interfere.

I don't know if it was politics, or some other reason, but Vic did not want to ask anyone in Haskell County for back-up and he needed someone to go with him to give the tough guy his chance. I got my rifle with the 30 round magazine and went with him. We spent the afternoon on and around the lease in question. I never saw the man to know which one he was, but for some reason the way he wanted to hunt his doves that day was the legal way. Every vehicle on the lease was parked, and the hunters were sitting or standing along the fence lines and shooting from there. Vic made sure every hunter on the lease knew we were there and available if anyone wanted to issue a challenge.

The game warden with the territory to the west of us was named Cecil Fox. He was stationed in Post, Texas. Cecil often came to Knox City to visit or confer with Vic. When he was in our area, he usually came by the Sheriff's office in Benjamin for a visit. He was the rattle snake expert in our area. He always kept a sack or two in his vehicle. One or more of the sacks almost always had one or more rattlers in them. Cecil's belt and holster were made of rattlesnake skin, and he made pen holders and paperweights of Lucite with snake rattles and fangs imbedded in them. He was something of a character and a delight to visit with.

One of his favorite things to do was to scare a passenger. After driving too fast for the passenger to bail, he would turn to him and advise him that he should sit "kinda light" because the sack under his feet had contained three little rattlers that morning. Cecil said he had looked when he stopped at the office but only saw two of them. The funny thing was that the better you knew the old rascal, the more likely you were to believe he might be telling the truth.

I was in the Sheriff's office one day when I received a call from a concerned citizen who said he was in Knox City and that a man, who I knew and had arrested previously, had been drinking enough to be affected. The citizen further said that this man had bought a pistol and announced he was going to go to Benjamin and kill me. He was believed to be leaving Knox City as the informant called. I knew the vehicle the man drove. I do not remember if there was no one available for back-up or if I just did not want to involve anyone else in the matter.

I left the office immediately, and drove toward Knox City to meet this man. I met him a short distance south of the Brazos River and turned around on him. He was driving erratically. I intended to stop him on the basis of the telephone call anyway, but this gave me additional cause. I stopped him and approached his vehicle with my hand on my gun ready to react in case he attempted to follow through on his reported threat. His window was down, and I told him he was weaving on the road. I asked him if he had been drinking. There was not a gun in sight. He admitted that he had a beer or two, and I asked for his driver's license. When he raised up to get his wallet from his back pocket I could see the gun. It had been pushed under his right thigh. I did not take his license, but asked him if he had been on his way to Benjamin to see me. He shook his head no. I then told him I could see a gun under his leg and asked him what he intended to do with it. He did not answer. I let him sit a few seconds, then told him if he was not going to use the gun I was going to reach across and get it. I advised him it would be a mistake to make any sudden movement while I was doing this. I then reached across him and took the gun. I then got him out of the car, and arrested him. I took him to the county jail. I did not file any charges regarding the gun, but did file either DUI or public intoxication.

During my 26-year career as a law enforcement officer, I never filed charges against a citizen for carrying a gun. I knew there was a state statute prohibiting the carrying of a hand gun, but I believed at that time, and still believe, this statute was unconstitutional. As a U.S. Border Patrolman, I arrested aliens who were in the United States illegally and in possession of firearms. This was a federal violation and the Bureau of Alcohol Tobacco tax and Firearms has responsibility of prosecution in these cases. I turned all such cases to this agency. I do not believe the second amendment right to possess and bear arms extends to illegal aliens.

★ Chapter Ten ★

Earlier I wrote about the cars I drove while at Benjamin and mentioned a chase I won. This was not always the case because I was driving the 1961 Ford. I was working in the Goree area one night with the constable, and we stopped a car suspected of containing some stolen items. As soon as we got out of my vehicle, the car took off again; the race was on. He took to the local oil field roads, which he knew as well as I did. His car had better acceleration than mine and my higher top end capability did no good on back roads. I had to drive deeper into the curves and corners and brake harder to stay with him.

The race ended in his favor when my brakes faded. If you have never experienced this condition, you are probably considerably younger than I am. We now have disc-type brakes standard in all cars that I know of, but at that time, cars used a brake drum system, rather than a rotor. If you got them too hot, they would reach the point where, no matter how hard you pressed on the brake pedal, the car would not stop.

We knew where the subject lived and waited for him there, but by the time we found him again, his car was as clean as a hound's tooth. If he had stolen items, they were well hidden. After disc type brakes became the standard for cars, brake fade mostly disappeared. I don't believe I have ever experienced brake fade with the system used today.

I lost another race in an unusual way. It began as I red-lighted a car just east of Knox City one night. He also ran and also took to the dirt roads in an attempt to dust me out. This race hardly got started before it was over. We came to a sharp right curve and the dust was thick as it was a dry period in the summer. I was about one hundred yards behind the Chevrolet car. I made the right curve and saw red lights on a road which teed back to the left just a very short distance ahead. This was a square corner, and I was already committed to taking it when I saw tail lights pop out of a dip in the road. I instantly realized it was the car I was after, but it was too late. I had to take the corner. The first lights a saw were the big round lights of a Ford, and it was probably a young couple who parked there and took off when they saw us approaching.

By the time I got stopped, backed up and back on the right road, the race was over. The Chevrolet had escaped. I knew who the Chevrolet belonged to and felt a lot better about the loss after I handled the fellow for something else a few months later and we talked about the race. He said that although he escaped, he still lost because his car wound up in a field near Rhineland with a blown motor.

I remember one of the things H.C. told me after I started working for him was that you can't give the people of an area more law enforcement than they will accept. I guess you could also say that an area generally gets about the level of law enforcement it deserves. Perhaps a better statement would be if a community wants good law enforcement, they not only have to find good law enforcement officers, but they have to support them.

I had been working for Knox County only a few months when I testified at my first trial. I arrested this fellow several times while there and do not remember the exact details of the first arrest. I do remember that it was for public intoxication and disorderly conduct, a minor misdemeanor. It was a Justice of the Peace trial with six jurors. I was the only witness and stated the reason, the circumstances of the arrest, and the reasons I believed him to have been intoxicated. The foreman of the jury was a local business owner and the others were all solid citizens of the community. I am sure that any one of them would have said he was all for law and order. In this case, however, they chose to disregard my testimony and found him not guilty, even though he presented no defense.

One of the jurors told me a few days after the trial not to feel bad about it. They all knew the man was guilty. They just decided to give him another chance. I was just getting acquainted in the community and trying to fit in. If that was the way they wanted the law enforced in the community, then that was okay by me. I continued to study the law and court decisions and get settled into the job. Several months passed until, one evening, the phone rang and it was the businessman who was foreman of the jury in the trial. He said this same fellow was drunk and needed to be arrested. That the fellow was in his store this time was the only difference. It would have been exactly the same situation as the first arrest, leaving me in the same situation as the first time.

I told him that since he knew I was not capable of telling when this man was drunk and rather than having me make another mistake, he should go to the Justice of the Peace and swear out a warrant for the fellow's arrest and I would be glad to arrest the man for him. I never heard anything else about this, but this was a small town and I know word got around. I never had another jury disregard my testimony in a local case. I did business with this man and we were on good terms the rest of my time in Knox County.

Sometimes, in order to do a good job of law enforcement it is necessary to do a lot of work knowing that, even if you are successful, it's going to feel like you are not accomplishing much. Such was the case in closing out a house burglary that occurred in Knox City. A young couple had moved in recently and there had been a house-warming party. Shortly thereafter, the house was ransacked and a lot of items, including silverware, a television, serving trays and a good number of things, were taken. We worked this case along with the Chief of Police of Knox City. I took our fingerprint kit and tried to lift prints, but got a lot of partials and smudges. In checking to see who the guests at the house warming were, we discovered that one was a known thief and burglar who was there with his wife. The victims knew the pair casually, but apparently were not aware of their background.

The Chief at Knox City did some good work on this and soon learned that it would be worth his time to go to the Big Springs, Midland area since the known burglar had been spending some time there. He believed he had a good chance of finding the stolen items in one of the pawn shops in that area.

His information was right on the money. He not only found the items in question, he got a copy the burglar's driver's license, which had been made by the pawn shop when he sold the items there. The man clearly had not believed any of us would check so far afield. The warrant was issued and he was arrested.

His wife had been known to jigger (act as look-out) for him for years. We were sure she helped him in this case, but we didn't have a shred of evidence to support such a belief. We learned that she was in Wichita Falls in the county jail serving out a hot check charge. The victim's friends had been told that we dusted for prints and at least some of them had visited the wife in Wichita Falls. I believed she knew about the dusting, but nobody except for us knew that we had nothing usable.

I had to be in Wichita Falls on another matter and decided to talk with his wife to see what her attitude was. She denied having anything to do with the burglary or even knowing her husband had done the job. The longer I talked to her, the more I became convinced she was lying. I decided to try a bluff. I told her it took two weeks to get fingerprint results back from the FBI and that if she was telling the truth she had nothing to worry about, but that if she saw me again she would know she was in trouble. As I left, I checked to see what day she would be discharged there and it fit pretty well with my bluff. I went back to Wichita Falls on the day she was to be released, and when the deputy opened the door to the cell, she saw me and became agitated. When I said, "Well, I guess you knew I would be back," she began to cry and admitted everything.

I had known from day one that even if I made a case against her, the best I could hope for was probation and that is exactly what I got: five years. That was not the way I liked to make a case, but, in her case, it was the only way. Probation does have conditions that, if not met, can lead to prison. The last I heard of her she was meeting the terms of her probation.

★ Chapter Eleven ★

As I became more familiar with the county, I began to realize that there were actually more communities than I had first realized. The extra community consisted of the criminal element. I had always known there was a criminal element, of course, but had always thought of a couple of burglars here and a thief or two there. It was not until I had been in law enforcement for some time that I realized these people actually constituted a community and, although they had no government, they knew each other, frequented the same dives, had the same interests, and often shared information.

I learned a lot of this from a man who was a professional criminal. He had relatives in our county and first came to my attention when we found a car that had been stolen in Ft. Worth and abandoned in our county. He had served time in prison and was still under twenty-five years of age at that time. I found an empty whiskey bottle with good prints on it under the seat of the car. I lifted them and called the Police Department in Fort Worth and talked with one of the detectives. I told him that I had prints and a good suspect, but he was not interested in coming after neither the car nor the suspect. It seemed the car belonged to a known prostitute and he didn't think she would testify against the man. All she wanted was her car back.

This fellow came front and center again about a year later when the night watchman in Knox City wrote down a license number of a strange car in an alley near a grocery store. Later in the night, he found the store had been broken into and the car was gone. I told him by radio how to cover the tracks in the alley until we could get either a cast or pictures. The license plate number convinced me the car would go to Lubbock, so I called the police department there and gave the description and license number of the car and asked them to hold it if located.

Right on schedule, Lubbock Police Department called and said they had the car, the money from the burglary, and three occupants. I asked them to make roll out prints of the car tires and went to Lubbock and brought them back. His partners made bond and were released, but he couldn't make bond, and was held pending indictment for burglary. This fellow and I came to know each other and got along well. He was not violent and presented no threat, so was made a trustee. He was a treasure trove of information. He knew the criminal community in both Lubbock and Fort Worth and would often tell me when a certain vehicle was in town and was good for a burglary, car theft, or other crime. He would also tell me the name of the owner of the vehicle. He liked me and appreciated being given trustee status. Although I was suspicious of the information at first, I soon learned that he was giving dependable information.

The burglary he was convicted of yielded only a few hundred dollars. I asked him once why he did not turn to robbery instead because it is much more profitable than working all night on a burglary. He said he knew that, but was scared to death of the penalty for robbery. I got a letter from him written from prison two or three years after I had moved to South Texas, thanking me for the way I had treated him and saying he was to be released from prison soon, had arranged for a job, and was going to go straight after his release. Apparently his relatives in Knox County had gotten my address for him. I never heard of him again and hoped he made it.

Now that I'm thinking about it, I also got a letter about that same time from one of the boys who we handled as a juvenile who had been considered a good prospect to end up in prison at one time. He also thanked me for setting him on the road to being a useful citizen. He had entered the military and was the driver for a high ranking officer, happy in his work, and had a good future lined up.

I've previously mentioned a couple of cases that were made by causing the suspect to come to an incorrect conclusion. Our investigative techniques resulted in their giving us information which they probably wouldn't have divulged if they had known how little actual evidence we had against them. This tactic was used very seldom by myself and other deputies. I have mentioned that the criminal community shared information. That included their assessment of the law enforcement people they came in contact with and an officer who was known to welch on an agreement or a promise with an informant or suspect would soon find himself unable to obtain the time of day when trying to obtain information from members of this community.

In the cases I have previously mentioned, the suspects were not actually lied to but misdirected, and even then they never knew that they'd reached a wrong conclusion. In everyday dealings with the shady side of our citizenry, I was scrupulously honest. This made it much easier to talk to most of these people. They knew they wouldn't be double-crossed or exposed if they talked to me in confidence. This made it much more likely that I could come up with a usable lead in almost any major crime in our community. I was as careful to maintain this reputation in the criminal community as I was to maintain a good credit rating in the business community.

I mentioned earlier that we had Braceros in the county. This was a program that gave temporary legal status to workers from Mexico. These workers were housed in barracks located in various places around the county. These barracks would house from a few to a hundred people. Of course, with that many extra people in the county there were some problems with them, but mostly thefts and intoxication. Ours was a dry county and the only source of beer or whiskey was bootleggers. It was not unusual for a couple of men to take a trunk full to a barracks in our county and sell it to the men housed there. They occasionally brought a prostitute or two in addition to the alcohol. This added to our workload during the months when they were present.

The Bracero program ended in 1964 and although the Braceros were admitted for a specific period of time and were expected to depart the country when their visas expired, some of them absconded and others came back as illegals shortly after the program ended.

There was a Border Patrol station in Lubbock which was responsible for enforcement of the immigration laws in our area and although we had seen these officers occasionally prior to

1964, they became more active in our area after the Braceros left. The more I saw these officers, the more I was convinced they were my kind of people. I talked to the men out of Lubbock and liked what I learned. This was an elite group and the Border Patrol was difficult to get into as less than ten percent of the people who applied successfully completed the academy and the first year's probationary period. The retirement system was better than what I had as a county officer and although it would be a tough first year, the men in Lubbock thought I could handle it and encouraged me to apply for entry. I finally decided to give it a try.

Part Two:
The U.S. Border Patrol

★ Chapter Twelve ★

I had been out of school a long time and following the Lubbock officers' advice, I brushed up on English grammar since part of the entry test consisted of an aptitude test to determine if the applicant could learn the Spanish language. I took the civil service examination in Abilene, Texas and passed. I was then scheduled to take a physical examination at the Goodfellow AFB in San Angelo, Texas. I passed the physical, but it was conditioned that I have some dental work completed. I was also given an oral examination by a board of senior Border Patrol officers. This was to give these men a chance to look the applicant over. The questions were designed to determine how he would handle certain situations, overall judgment, and the ability to think on his feet.

I passed and was accepted pending completion of the required dental work. This delayed my entry as I had to wait until the first call up after my dental work was completed. I did this as soon as possible and sent the dentist's affidavit as soon as I could get all of the dental work completed. I received notice that I was to report to the Border Patrol sector headquarters in Del Rio, Texas, on May 1, 1967.

Although my resignation was effective May 1, 1967, H.C. would not hear of taking our children out of school and there were still a few weeks until end of term. I went to Del Rio while Sylvia remained in the living quarters in the jail and the kids stayed in school until the end of the school year. That was the kind of man he was. I had his support all through the process of joining the Border Patrol.

After a brief orientation period, I bought a uniform and leather and became a member of the Border Patrol station at Eagle Pass, Texas. My academy class was not due to report until mid-June. I found a motel room near the Border Patrol station in Eagle Pass and went to work as a trainee in a brand new world. As I had driven east from Del Rio to Eagle Pass with the Rio Grande just a short distance to my right, I was seeing palm trees, some with dates hanging in clusters. I thought this must be a tropical paradise.

The first thing I learned was that, in Eagle Pass, the morning sun came up in the north. That's right, the river runs more to the south there than it does to the east. Even after realizing this, I still had to fight to keep things straight as the sun still rose in the north every morning. The next thing I learned was right along the river the area was verdant with a tropical appearance because of irrigation. A short distance away was ranch country with little irrigation. That area was brush country and everything either stung, bit, or had thorns.

The brush was full of things that I had never seen before: huajilla, guayacan (Mexican ironwood), black brush, white brush, cat claw, and a myriad of other plants I was not familiar with as well as birds and animals. There were grackles, cara cara birds which look like a miniature eagle with their white heads, and an occasional green jay. There were javelinas, indigo, and coral snakes, and an occasional cougar track on the drag strips where illegal aliens crossed the border. A coating of loose soil was maintained on these strips by dragging a device made of large tractor tires that was too wide to jump across. This forced a person crossing to leave evidence of their crossing. These strips were checked every morning by slowly driving and checking for indications of persons crossing. This operation was called cutting for sign and the men were sign cutters.

The other major operation of the Eagle Pass Border Patrol station was traffic check. We searched vehicles traveling away from the border area to assure that all occupants were legally in the country. Traffic check was done in two ways. One way was to set up traffic cones, red lights, and stop signs and stop and searched all vehicles that drove the road leaving the border area. There were not enough men assigned to the station to cover all roads in this manner, so roving patrols were used. A roving patrol is when a vehicle and two men either patrol the road or park at the side and look over passing traffic, stopping the vehicles that seem most likely to contain illegal aliens.

There were quite a few favorite points used to make illegal crossings into the United States. These crossings were known and marked on our maps and given numbers so that we could quickly respond to information that a crossing was being used for illegal entry. There were also favorite spots on the river bank on the U.S. side from which these crossings could be observed. I liked the river watch operations and, after I completed probation, that's where I often was when not specifically assigned to another operation.

We trainees were all assigned to work with a journeyman patrol officer in whatever capacity we were working. While waiting the six weeks for our academy to begin, we gained some knowledge of what we would be doing after we successfully completed it.

I managed to find time for one weekend trip back to Benjamin to see the wife and children before the academy began. Sylvia had arranged to store the furniture and household goods and was prepared to spend much of the summer with her mother in Oklahoma City while I wasn't there. Housing was at a premium in Eagle Pass and, to be sure we had suitable quarters, I rented a house before I went to the academy. This made our finances tight the rest of the summer but we had a suitable place to live and stayed there the entire time we lived in Eagle Pass. Sylvia moved the family into the house before school began and was ready for the school year.

Meanwhile, I entered the Border Patrol Academy with the other men from our station, one of whom was a young man from Knox County, Texas, where I had worked for the last six years. We were acquainted, but only casually. The guys at the Eagle Pass station laughingly told me to be careful not to drop a pencil because I would be two days behind by the time I picked it up; I soon found out that they were only half-joking. The subjects were immigration law, Spanish, self-defense, firearms, and, for those of us who did not already know Spanish, a long list of Spanish vocabulary words each evening after classes.

The academy was an abandoned coast guard station a few miles out of Port Isabel, Texas. My roommate was a bright, well-organized, young man of twenty-five years from Boise, Idaho, who had married shortly before he entered the Border Patrol. He was doing well and I believe would have finished well up in the scholastic standings, but when we got into firearms training five weeks into what was to be about a fifteen week course, he resigned. He had doubts that he would have the mental toughness to shoot another human even to save his or a partner's life. I liked the young fellow and hated to see him go, but I thought he made the right decision. I certainly wouldn't want to work with a partner I couldn't depend to back me all the way when things went south.

I was nearing my thirty-eighth birthday (which passed while I was in the academy) and had been out of school a long time. My recent studying of state law and court decisions helped greatly, and I soon was organized to the point that I finished the academy third in my class overall. We were scheduled to have the graduation proceedings, but hurricane Beulah took dead aim at the Port Isabel area and the academy was evacuated until after the hurricane had passed.

I and most of the other men stationed at Eagle Pass went back there until after the hurricane. We returned to the Academy to find the buildings in shambles. We stayed a couple of days helping put tar paper on the roofs of the living quarters of the instructors. They experienced wind gusts of more than one hundred and twenty-five miles per hour. The graduation ceremonies were cancelled and we returned to our stations. Instead of receiving my letter of commendation for my third place finish from a commissioner of immigration at a graduation ceremony, it was handed to me by the Deputy Chief of the Del Rio Sector. Our class was the only one ever graduated by a hurricane.

★ Chapter Thirteen ★

We had finished the Academy and there was nothing but smooth sailing ahead, right? Wrong! We would be on probation until the first year was complete. In addition, we would have advanced classes at Sector Headquarters once a week and be tested at the five and a half month and the ten month mark. We would be observed every day by a journeyman officer who would be in a position to write us up either good or bad, depending on his evaluation of our field work.

We soon lost one man from our class. He was assigned to work a remote area with a journeyman and they stopped for coffee on the way out of town. The trainee brought a large-mouth thermos containing soup for his lunch, but had forgotten to bring a spoon with which to eat it. Instead of asking the waitress for a plastic spoon or asking the journeyman to stop at a convenience store so he could buy one, he just stuck one of the cafe's silver spoons in his pocket. This thoughtless act reflected badly on his character and on the Border Patrol in general. His journeyman wrote the incident up and it was adios trainee.

I learned right away that if I wanted lunch, I would have to bring it with me to work. The same applied to water. A gallon thermos of cold water was an absolute necessity. A trique (personal items, tools, utensils) bag or box was also needed. Some of the men carried a small overnight canvas bag, but I settled on a .50 caliber ammo box from a military surplus store. It was waterproof, and would hold extra ammo, pliers, survival-type knife, first-aid kit, screwdrivers, key ring or chain, lunch, and other small items. I still have the first one I bought. It traveled more than one million miles with me, probably more than two or three million. It still travels with me on trips.

The U.S. Border Patrol had what we believed was the best language lab in the country for Spanish. Even so, after fourteen weeks of intensive study and instruction, we were still far from fluent when we graduated. We did, however, have the basis to finish learning the language and needed only to increase our vocabularies and practice until we could conjugate the verbs without having to stop and think about person and tenses all through a sentence. I set about learning the language by continuing to increase my vocabulary and practicing as much as I reasonably could. By the time I passed my ten month examination, I had progressed to the point where I could do the required paperwork in processing a person who had been apprehended and was being removed from the country. I had finally settled into the job and knew I intended to make it a career.

Even though I had successfully completed probation and could now speak enough Spanish to get along, nothing could prepare me for everything a Border Patrolman might encounter.

We apprehended a group of aliens who had just that day crossed the Rio Grande and were walking north. We took them to headquarters for processing and were just getting started when one of the patrolmen started laughing and saying, "Hey, guys, come and hear this." Several men approached to see what was going on. He told me to ask this guy his name. His answer convulsed the group into laughter. He said his name was "Hoonior Honnes." It took me a minute to get it but, while the others laughed, I figured out that he had just told us his name was Junior Jones. Everyone thought he was yanking our chain and two or three of the guys took a turn at finding out who he really was, but he was adamant. No amount of questioning as to his parentage (his mother was a prostitute, his father unknown) could shake his story. His mother had told him his name was Junior Jones and that was that as far as he was concerned. Finally, his companions were questioned and confirmed that they knew him as Junior Jones. He was processed and returned to Mexico.

By the time I made probation, I had done all the various operations performed at Eagle Pass and formed my preference and opinions. We had one semi-permanent checkpoint. Lack of personnel prevented manning it 24/7 and, even when it was operating, there was not enough personnel to block the other available roads, leaving at least one avenue of travel that could be used to smuggle aliens out of our area. Even when the station was manned, there was no regular backup operation to prevent a smuggler from letting his aliens out just over a hill some three or four hundred yards short of us, letting them walk around through the pasture, and picking them up further down the road a mile or so. Those of us who were assigned to work this point at night often drove back toward town the next morning along the fence to see how many loads had walked around us while we stood checking the cars which came through.

I am not saying this to be critical of anyone. I don't know what the supervisor in charge of the station had to deal with from his superiors or what his thinking was. I am just stating facts as I saw them. I decided that any smuggler who pulled up to that point with a load of aliens in his vehicle should be able to beat the case on a plea of insanity. I do know that, by 1969, the supervisor of our station was getting heat from upstairs. Illegal aliens were being found in the Chicago area and, upon questioning, were telling the investigators that they were one of a load of 40 to 50 persons who had been hauled out of the Eagle Pass area.

★ Chapter Fourteen ★

The young man from Knox County and I were assigned a 4:00 p.m. to midnight roving patrol shift on one of the secondary highways I thought was used to haul all of these big loads. I knew how I wanted to work it and my partner agreed. We built a blind, or hide, by augmenting small bushes twenty-five yards into the pasture next to a culvert over a draw that was high enough that we could park under it. We took stools to sit on and, during the daytime, hid our vehicle under the culvert and sat behind the brush, watching the road. We stopped few vehicles during the day as we could eliminate almost all because we were not stopping anything that could not haul a large number of people.

After dark, we moved to a nearby ranch entrance where we parked the car far enough off the highway that it could not be seen by a passing vehicle. One man stayed with the car and the other went near the road where he could get a good look at passing traffic. When a suitable vehicle passed, the one at the road would signal with his flashlight and the car would come forward and pick him up, and the vehicle would be pursued and stopped.

We maintained this operation for two weeks without a single arrest, but we could see cars passing during the afternoon that we were sure were running the road to see if it was clear. After two weeks, we had almost completed a shift and were about ready to go to headquarters when we got a radio message asking that we hold position as an informant just called and said a group of twenty-six aliens had just left a hotel in Piedras Negras walking downriver and were supposed to cross nearby. This sounded like what we had spent the last two weeks working toward, so we stayed put and were ready to roll if they came up.

About an hour-and-a-half later, a two-ton truck with a box bed about six feet deep passed and we fell on it. Bingo! That was our vehicle and Eagle Pass had caught its first big load. There were 42 aliens and a driver. My partner and I held the load until other units could come and help us move it to headquarters for processing. After help arrived, one Border Patrolman drove the truck and another sat on the back of the cab with a twelve gauge riot gun and held the smuggled aliens in the bed of the truck until we arrived at headquarters. The processing lasted through the night and much of the next day. The case was given to those responsible for handling the prosecution.

The young patrolman who worked with me on this operation was Tony Hobert, a resident of Knox County and fellow academy graduate. Tony is now retired and still lives in Munday, Texas. I called him to see how his memory corresponded with mine on this case and the only difference was that he thought there were 43 aliens and the driver. Tony said he has a vivid memory of climbing up and looking into the truck with his flashlight and seeing a sea of eyes looking back at him. He was the man who sat on the back of the cab and held the aliens in the bed of the truck as they were being transported to the headquarters. He said when he sat on the cab as they started back to town, he worked the action of the riot gun and when the aliens heard the clack-clack of the action, everyone's eyes got even larger and fixed on him.

Another way to watch for aliens was by river or line watch. There was a spur rail line that ran from Mexico through Eagle Pass and some thirty miles to the north to Spofford, Texas. This line connected with the Southern Pacific rail line that had been completed in 1883 to establish a southern route to the west coast and was a main object of the Gadsden Purchase. The railroad bridge across the Rio Grande between Eagle Pass, Texas, and Piedras Negras, Mexico, had a gate in the middle which was closed and locked except when trains went through. It was supposed to prevent foot traffic, but could be easily defeated as there was a gap a person could slip through. There was a walkway beside the rails to allow for customs inspections of arriving trains. The only lighting I remember was from the light of the cities on each side of the river. It was so dark a person could sit or lay down alongside the walk and not be seen by the person passing on the walkway.

Border Patrolmen doing line watch operations often set up on the bridge after dark. I was in the office one night when a patrolman brought in three females he had caught crossing the railroad bridge. This was not uncommon as females often crossed from Mexico to the U.S. side to work the various bars along the streets near the river. The girls were giggling and the officer had a red face. I didn't hear the question and answer, but the story was soon going around. One of the officers asked the girls what was so funny. They told him the officer had been lying beside the walkway and as they passed, reached out and grabbed one of them by the ankle. She screamed like El Diablo himself had her and had wet his arm almost to the shoulder.

I was watching the river one afternoon, working alone near the landfill for the city of Eagle Pass. A lone man appeared on the Mexican side walking upstream toward the crossing. He was carrying an opaque plastic bag over his shoulder and a smaller mesh bag in one hand. The plastic bag had enough transparency that I could see it contained a green substance. I thought I was about to make my first Border Patrol marijuana case. It became apparent the man was going to cross where I thought and I moved to a position where I could intercept him far enough from the river to assure an apprehension.

My plan was flawless and I scared the poor fellow half to death. He was a legal resident of the U. S. and the opaque bag contained an avocado seedling, while the mesh bag contained a game rooster. The law required that any person wishing to enter the U.S. present himself for inspection at a designated port of entry. I took the man to the port of entry and had him present himself as required. He was admitted to the U.S., but his avocado plant was seized by the U.S. Department of Agriculture and his rooster was quarantined. Thus ended my first—almost—marijuana case as a Border Patrolman.

★ CHAPTER FIFTEEN ★

Most people who come to the border in the Eagle Pass area come from the north through the scenic Texas Hill Country. They drive across the Edwards Plateau and drop down into the Texas Brush Country which appears barren and featureless. I soon found that it was teeming with life. Deer were numerous, as were raccoons, coyotes, opossums, javelina, bobcats, an occasional cougar and a myriad of smaller wildlife. Golden eagles (for which the Eagle Pass area was named) migrated across the river and back. At least three kinds of dove, quail, and waterfowl were plentiful in the cooler months.

By this time, my oldest son, Steven, was an accomplished predator caller and an excellent marksman, and his younger brother, David, was catching up. Looking for a place to hunt, the boys approached a small ranch outside town and asked the lady who answered the door for permission to hunt. She started to refuse, then learned they wanted to call for coyotes and bobcats. She told them they were awfully young, but if they thought they could get rid of some of the predators which had been decimating her flock of chickens and catching her cats, she would give them a try.

They went on by the house into the ranch and when they stopped by on the way back to town, they opened the trunk and showed the lady it was full. They had two or three coyotes and a bobcat in just a few hours of calling. The lady not only invited them to come back as often as they could, she passed the word to her friends and the problem of finding a place for them to hunt was solved as long as we lived in Eagle Pass.

The man in charge of the Brush Crew was a supervisory patrolman in his fifties and a fine man to work for. Due to personnel shortage, his crew usually amounted to five or six men at a time. Most of the time, they could work only one trail at a time, even when there were more. By trails, I mean where sign had been found showing illegal entrants crossing at a river crossing or a drag strip and leaving a trail of tracks or other sign toward further entry into the U. S.

The usual way to work this was to start a couple of men following the sign and have the other units cut for sign ahead in the direction they were going. The Border Patrol had their own pilots and planes at that time and we could usually obtain the help of a pilot flying a Super Cub. The walkers would have handy-talkies and the pilot would make pass after pass in the plane over the walkers and on out the direction they were walking. If the units ahead of the walkers found the sign ahead of them on a trail, road, or fence line, that unit would take up the trail and the walkers would then become sign cutters ahead of the new walkers.

One of three things would happen: the aliens would be caught, the trail would be lost, or darkness would make it impossible to follow the sign further. It was not unusual to apprehend two or three groups of aliens in a day. The pilots were all ex-patrolmen and knew what was happening on the ground. More often than not, they would spot the aliens ahead of the walkers and end the chase in short order. It was also not unusual to dispose of all fresh trails and get the aliens processed by noon or earlier. When this happened, we would go look for more signs, watch the river, or just explore the area. You can't be too familiar with the area you are responsible for. This was my favorite type of work available in the Eagle Pass area. Having been raised a farm boy, making my spending money by trapping and selling fur, I felt comfortable doing this work.

I never knew what we would find next, but most of the people were from Mexico and entering the U.S. to find work. I remember one group of seven or eight people we found walking almost parallel to the river and some seven or eight miles inland. They had crossed the water a short distance upriver from Laredo and had been walking for five days. When asked where they thought they were, they said they should be almost to San Antonio and were amazed and disgusted to learn they were still less than ten miles from Mexico. As the river runs more north and south than it does east and west in that area, it only took a little misdirection to cause them to make a big mistake. Many groups would have a compass with them, but these boys did not.

I remember working a trail going from the Eagle Pass area toward Uvalde one day. It was a hot summer day and one of the patrolmen found this group at about noon resting in the shade beside a pond. They saw him coming and fled like a heard of deer. We called for a plane, and worked most of the afternoon until the pilot finally spotted them ahead of us, and we converged on the spot he indicated. They were hidden in the brush in an area of a half-acre or so, and we began digging them out one by one. I came to one backed under a small tree in thick brush and reached for him, catching him by the front of the shirt at the shoulders and pulling him forward. He gave up and stood with me still holding him to make sure he would not run again. He stood up and up, and suddenly I was standing on tiptoe with my arms stretched overhead. This was the biggest alien I had ever seen. He was about six feet, eight inches tall and would have weighed well over 230 lbs. When I patted him down for weapons, his legs felt like cedar posts. I sure was glad he wasn't a fighter as I wouldn't have lasted long enough to yell for help if he attacked.

While I was fitting into my job and improving my Spanish skills, things were not going so well for the rest of the family. Sylvia was a fair redhead, and many of the clerks in the various stores around town did not speak English. When they saw her moving in their direction, they would quickly find something else to do. She was having trouble getting waited on downtown. By the end of the first year, it was becoming all too clear that the school system wasn't providing the education we wanted for our children. I liked my position and I got along well with the men with whom I worked, but, as time went by, it became clear that the best thing I could do was to look for an opportunity to transfer to a station which had better schools. This was not going to be quick or easy as there was not much movement in the patrol at that time. I started keeping an eye out for an opening and let it be known at sector headquarters that I was interested in a transfer. There was nothing to do then except wait for an opening to appear.

In the meantime, there was plenty to do in the Eagle Pass

Station. Smuggling activity was increasing, and I was often working roving patrol looking for vehicles hauling illegal aliens. One such occasion occurred when a trainee and I were working the roads downriver from Eagle Pass. We were observing traffic on Farm to Market Road 2644 when we encountered a car towing a U-Haul trailer following another car. This was late in the evening and traffic was light. It was almost certainly a smuggling case, so I red-lighted the car and trailer. A quick check showed the trailer was loaded with some fifteen aliens. I quickly helped my partner secure this load then left him to guard this rig while I attempted to catch the other vehicle, which I believed would contain the actual smugglers.

I got on the radio to get the vehicle stopped at Carrizo Springs. I got lucky and found a game warden on duty and already on the road ahead of me. He stopped and held the vehicle for me. My partner and I took everything to headquarters. We made the case and sent it up for prosecution.

The unusual thing about this case was that, after the prosecution, people began talking with the two men who were in the lead car. They told the officers that when the trailer rig was stopped, they suspected they would also be stopped and had put the money they had collected from the people they were smuggling, some 2,500 dollars, into a handkerchief, tied it up, and thrown it out the car window shortly before they were stopped. Two days had passed before we learned this, and, although we drove the area twice looking for the handkerchief, we didn't find it. We were satisfied that if the story was true, then the money had already been found and removed.

★ Chapter Sixteen ★

The river crossing near the city landfill continued to be my favorite area from which to watch the river. I had been working at Eagle Pass for over two years and was watching that area often. On one occasion, I was working evenings with a trainee, and we saw a group of four men come upriver on the Mexican side of the river and lay up across the crossing we were watching. This was shortly before sundown. We were sure they would cross after dark, so I put my trainee in some Carrizo cane which grew in abundance in that area, away from the river bank twenty-five yards while I concealed myself, also in the cane, ten yards from the top of the river bank. The top of the bank was thirty feet higher than the water and a trail sloped steeply upward with a step or two carved out in the steepest places.

The plan was to let the crossers walk past me. Then, I would come behind and challenge them when my partner would break cover in front of them. We should have control of the situation by the time they recovered from their surprise. They crossed right on schedule but when the lead man was about even with me, he suddenly stopped and began a whispered conference. They suddenly panicked and broke back for the river. They hit that steep bank at a run. I could hear them tumbling down the bank, grunting every time they hit the ground, followed by several splashes as some of them went all the way to the water.

After it was clear they had gone back to Mexico, I looked at the trail where they fell down. It was littered with cans of sardines, tortillas, homemade cheese, shirts, shoes, and other items, showing they had provisioned for several days of walking. I never knew for sure what spooked them. It was a moonlit night, and I always thought the trainee had gotten anxious, moved, and they saw a glint of light from his highly polished badge or name plate.

I continued to watch this area and made one of the two biggest cases of my stay in Eagle Pass. I was watching this crossing from my favorite blind one afternoon, again with a trainee. We saw two men come upriver on the Mexico side, but, instead of stopping at the place crossers usually prepared to cross, these two went upriver some three hundred yards and began to get ready to cross. We quickly got in the vehicle and I drove around the landfill to the area where I thought they would appear. It was a pasture area with mesquite and brush. Visibility was limited from thirty to forty yards through the brush. I parked the vehicle behind some heavy brush and found us a good area. We got some ten yards apart and waited to see if they would come our way. We were four hundred yards from the river, and there was no regularly used trail through this area. Fortune smiled on us that day. Not only did they come through the area, they came directly at us.

They were walking close together and one was carrying something tied up in a white cloth. We stayed hidden until they were thirty feet away and then, on my signal, we both stepped out and I told them to halt. The one with the cloth bag ran for the river, and I told my trainee to take him. I was walking forward all the time and the one I was approaching shoved his hand into his front pocket. I could see a bulge there. I drew my own pistol. By this time, I was less than twenty feet from my man. I still had not seen the gun I was sure he had in his pocket, but my gun was pointed straight at his chest. I increased my pressure on the trigger and waited for him to show the gun. His sporting blood turned to pee, his eyes flared. He jerked his hand out of his pocket and put both hands above his head. I yelled at my partner who was out of sight to be careful, that this one had a gun, and he answered he had his man. I kept mine covered while I cuffed him, then confirmed what I already knew. The gun was a .32 caliber Galesi auto. The other front pocket had two condoms filled with a brownish substance and when I looked at him and asked what it was in Spanish, he replied "H" for heroin.

We loaded everything up and took it to the headquarters for processing. The items tied up in the white cloth proved to be a one-pound box of powdered sugar and an Ohaus balance scale and weights. Both men were aliens and had crossed illegally.

This was before the Drug Enforcement Agency was formed and the Customs Service Agency was responsible for enforcing and prosecuting violations of U.S. drug laws at that time. There were several agents assigned to their office in Eagle Pass and they was notified of the arrests. A couple of their agents came to our office after we had done the paperwork on the aliens. The Customs Service Agents weighed and tested the material in the condoms and confirmed that it was indeed heroin and although it had been cut once, it was still high quality and weighed forty-eight grams. We then turned the case over to them for prosecution.

The next day, a couple of Custom Service Agents came to me asking if I had information that had led to the arrest of the two men and related questions. They were worried about the possibility that a leak of some kind in their operations had resulted in my learning that the two men would be crossing into the U. S. with contraband. I assured them that the arrests were the result of the Border Patrol line watch operations and that, although I had seen the same two men previously in that area on the Mexico side of the river, this arrest was not a result of any inside information in my possession. I learned that their undies were bunched up because they had learned of a smuggling operation being run by the man who had the heroin in his pocket and had managed to get an undercover agent close enough to him that he was, at the time of our arrest, trying to make a buy of heroin from the subject who was living in the U.S. near Eagle Pass with his wife, who was a U.S. citizen.

They had subpoenaed the telephone records of this man and had learned he was a big-time operator with many customers over a large area of the U.S. The narcotics that my trainee and I seized were actually a sample he was taking to his house to show to their undercover agent who was attempting to set up a sting operation involving a larger quantity of the narcotic. The man we arrested with the scales and powdered sugar was actually the subject's bodyguard. I later had an opportunity to talk with this undercover agent and he said that while he would be talking with the subject and negotiating the buy, the bodyguard would sit or squat by the subject with a large caliber pistol in his belt and glare at the agent. I told him that the man could have had a gun in his belt when we fell on them in the pasture, but that, if he did, he had thrown it away during the chase before my trainee caught him after he ran from us.

Both the undercover agent and I testified at the trial, which was held at the federal courthouse in Del Rio, Texas. The smuggler received a sentence of ten years to serve in a federal prison and his bodyguard was given five years. The smuggler's wife was also charged, but her case was pending at that time and I was not involved. I never knew the disposition of the case against her.

UNITED STATES DEPARTMENT OF JUSTICE
IMMIGRATION AND NATURALIZATION SERVICE
U. S. Border Patrol - Hudson Drive
Del Rio, Texas - Dec. 7, 1981

DRT 40/802

Mr. Kenneth R. Lamascus
U. S. Border Patrol
Uvalde, Texas

Dear Mr. Lamascus:

Attached is a letter from the Regional Commissioner asking me to extend his sincere thanks to each officer involved in the recent Presidential security detail.

I join the Regional Commissioner in thanking you for your participation. Even though the working conditions were unpleasant and the hours were long, you performed your duties in a manner that was most impressive to me and to the other Agencies involved. One Supervisory Secret Service Agent made the comment that he has never worked with an organization that demonstrated a higher degree of professionalism.

Again, thanks from the Regional Commissioner and from me personally for a job well done.

Jack L. Richardson
Chief Patrol Agent

★ Chapter Seventeen ★

President Nixon did two things shortly after being elected that I remember. He dedicated the Lake Amistad Dam and Reservoir, meeting the president of Mexico in the middle of the dam for a joint ceremony. I worked my first presidential security detail during that meeting. I had previously worked security for an event featuring Governor Connally of Texas while I was a Deputy Sheriff in Knox County.

The event with President Nixon went off almost without incident. The two presidents were supposed to start from their respective sides of the dam and arrive in the middle at the same time. The Mexican president started before Nixon was ready while one of the Secret Service men was telling his Mexican counterpart in halting Spanish that the president had not started yet and the Mexican replied in perfect English, "Don't sweat the small stuff, man. We got it handled." At least there was no incident as far as the Mexican side was concerned and only a small delay at the center of the dam.

The other thing I remember Nixon did was create the Drug Enforcement Administration and initiate Operation Intercept, which was an attempt to close off the supply of marijuana coming across the river into the United States. It just about closed the border. Although I only saw a small section of this, I believe it was about the same all along the Mexico Border. We received an influx of people from all over the country, mostly customs inspectors and service agency people from the interior, almost none of whom had the foggiest idea of what it was like on the border. They were assigned to work as partners with those of us who were already there and the river crossings were watched, as well as units assigned to all roads leading away from the border.

My first partner from this group was a customs inspector from an eastern seaport. He had come to the wild, wild west fully prepared to do combat. He had his heavy gun on his belt (I do not remember if it was a government or personal gun). He had his hideout gun in an ankle holster and a bowie knife in a holster suspended between his shoulder blades. He knew about unauthorized pills, cargo holds, and the most likely place to find hidden hashish on a ship, but wild horses could not have pulled him three feet away from the pavement as he was terrified of rattlesnakes.

We were working roving patrol on a secondary road and he would stick his flashlight out of his window and carefully survey the side of the road before he would even get out at the edge of the pavement to relieve his bladder. I wondered what he would do if he actually saw a rattlesnake but was afraid to try to find him one because I didn't want to be near him when he did see one.

There was one serious incident in the first few days of this operation. One of our Border Patrolmen was assigned to work with a customs man from somewhere in the interior. He was assigned to work a traffic operation with one of the Border Patrolmen and they would be relieving another unit already at the assigned location. The Border Patrolman arrived at the office ready to go to work and it was time to relieve the other unit, but his partner from customs had not arrived at the office.

He called the motel where his partner was staying and, although the man answered the phone, the Border Patrolman could not make sense of what he said. He went on to relieve the unit on site and on the way called a supervisor on the radio and told him he was relieving the traffic check unit alone because his partner had not showed up and, when he called, he found the man incoherent.

I was on duty at the time and heard this radio call. When I arrived back at the end of my shift, I found the office full of supervisors from both customs and our people. I was told that sometime after I heard the radio call, the customs man had gone to where the Border Patrol officer was working. The officer pulled a gun on him and took him back to the station at gun point. There someone disarmed the customs agent and called supervisors.

I never knew all the details of the actions taken, but I never saw the customs man again and was told he had been sent home or at least somewhere else. I know I would not have worked with him under any circumstances and doubt any other Border Patrolman in our station would have either. By the end of the first week of Operation Intercept, the price of marijuana was rising and, had there been more available personnel, the operation could have been a resounding success, at least in my opinion. However, by this time, the President of Mexico was complaining because of the inconvenience dealt to his citizens in passing back and forth across the river, and it was becoming clear that not enough resources had been allocated to the operation. It was discontinued in less than a month and things were soon back to normal.

After Operation Intercept folded, we returned to normal operations and I continued to watch the river when we finished sign cutting early or any other opportunity arose. I remember working that area on an evening shift and saw four aliens go upriver past the landfill area, which was a considerable distance. It was about sundown and I could see them through my binoculars. The aliens were getting ready to cross in an area which would take them above the area where we had previously caught the heroin case.

I went to where I thought I would intercept them and hid my vehicle. There was a trail across a maize field which had been recently harvested and still had loose stalks and leaves scattered across the field. There was a pile of brush which had been piled at the edge of the field and the trail went right by it. I settled down behind the brush pile, expecting a 15 or 20 minute wait. After waiting some 30 minutes with no action, I was beginning to think I had guessed wrong about which trail they would use when I began to hear a very faint rustling in the field on the other side of my brush pile. By this time, it was fully dark and there was no moon. By the faint noise they were making, I thought they were being extra cautious and moving slowly.

Finally, the rustling sounded like it was just the other side of the brush, so I took a couple of long steps while simultaneously turning my flashlight on and commanding them to halt in Spanish. Well, the only thing wrong was that my flashlight was showing an empty field. I moved it side to side, still nothing. I looked down about where I had heard the noise and there I saw a skunk almost between my feet. The skunk had his tail raised and was looking back over his shoulder at me and the light. Being an old country boy from Oklahoma who had trapped coons, possums, and skunks as a boy, I knew I was in imminent danger of being sprayed. I kept the light in his eyes, and stood very, very still. It was a standoff for about 30 seconds which seemed like 5 minutes to me. Finally, the skunk waddled off and I went back to my vehicle and found something else to do for the rest of my shift. I have no idea what happened to the aliens that I had seen earlier.

It was not all work and no play in the Eagle Pass Station. There were hunters and fishermen in the station and there was a field not too far out of town where all Border Patrolmen were welcome to hunt doves in season. We took advantage of this and other opportunities as well. During dove hunting season, several men would meet at the field with a tree line around it and wait for passing doves. The birds were plentiful and a good shot could almost always get a limit. As a matter of fact, most days even one of the fellows who was not a good shot got his limit. His system was simple. He had seen my oldest son, Steven, shoot and found out that he was an excellent shooter who seldom missed. He talked Steven into shooting for him. He would sit on the tailgate of his pickup, drinking beer, give Steven ammunition, and Steven would shoot his limit for him. Most of us would then give our cleaned doves to one of the men who would put them in his freezer and keep them until we could get together and have a dove feast and beer bust.

I had a 5-horsepower outboard motor, and one of the men with whom I had become friends, had a fourteen foot Jon boat. There was a canal system through the area and it was full of channel catfish. He and I used to take a spinach basket full of quart beer bottles with some three feet of line tied to each and a small treble hook attached. We would bait with a stink bait, drop the baited rigs overboard and float down the canal at various points. We caught a lot of fish and had a fish fry from time to time.

Although Steven was now out of high school, the school system continued to be a problem. Sylvia and I were both concerned about the progress being made by the younger children. David was in junior high and two or three times a week brought homework assignments that I thought were ridiculous. When I helped him, we would spend four hours just getting his math homework done. I went to the principal with the assignment and showed it to him. He defended the teacher and went with me to talk to her.

She told me the kids all loved the homework and no one else had complained. The principal accepted this ridiculous statement without question, at least as long as I was there. Apparently, he had a heart-to-heart with the teacher after I left as the problem was corrected. This was typical of the problems, and they occurred faster than I could get them corrected.

There were about eight weeks left in the school year in 1970 when the sector Chief was in Eagle Pass one day and offered me a transfer to Uvalde. He said that he wanted to send someone to Uvalde who could get along with the supervisor of the station there, and he thought I could. Sylvia was jubilant. Although she had made some friends in the community of Border Patrol wives, she still hated the community and city of Eagle Pass. I accepted the transfer, and we began packing.

★ Chapter Eighteen ★

We moved to Uvalde with six weeks left in the school year and enrolled the kids in school. One of the first things we did was talk to the principal of the elementary school about where to put Randy, my youngest son, who was still having trouble with math. The principal placed him in a class taught by Larry Warren, who had Randy caught up to the rest of his class and making good grades before the end of the school year. Larry and his wife, Loretta, later became valued friends. Uvalde had a good school system and the other children were soon also doing well in school.

On the first day I was scheduled to work at the new station, I was picked up at home by the senior patrolman in charge of the station. He was also the only supervisor in the station. Another man and I had transferred from Eagle Pass to Uvalde at the same time and we made the fourth and fifth men in the station. On our way to the office on that first day, the senior informed me that he ran a "taut ship," thus giving me some indication of what the Chief was talking about when he offered me the transfer. The senior had no idea that day just how much slack I would jerk in the rigging of his ship over the years and I was to get pulled up short a few times myself. Although we most definitely had our differences over the years, we managed to work together and I am willing to call it a draw if he is. This is written not as an account about personalities or differences of opinion, but as an account of the highlights of my law enforcement career. Persons and personalities are mentioned only as they apply.

At the time I reported for duty, our office was two small rooms on the third floor of the Uvalde County Courthouse. Uvalde had been a two-man station, but, just a few months earlier, one man had transferred in from Comstock and was still getting settled in when we two from Eagle Pass got here. Uvalde was primarily a farm and ranch check station when we arrived. Farm and ranch checking involved going over the station area checking for anyone who was working illegally in the country.

The station was responsible for all of Uvalde and Real Counties and for part of Edwards County. During the first few months, I worked mostly with either the station Senior or the other man who had been here for quite some time. He was a farm and ranch specialist. At least, that was his preference. I was told the men at the station where he worked prior to Uvalde had called him "Vitamin" due to the fact that he so often brought in only one alien, but did so almost every day. He liked to slowly patrol along the various roads in the territory, checking for any activity which might involve the possibility of people doing the work being illegally employed.

The area south of the Edwards Plateau had some rich, irrigated farm land in the Uvalde, Knippa, and Sabinal areas and one only had to look across the fields to locate possible violations. At that time, during the time when various crops were being harvested, there would be loads of people hauled into our area from Eagle Pass by labor contractors. They would furnish transportation and locate fields to harvest, charging the workers a fee for their services. We had a few contractors who were local and housed their workers wherever they could find space for sleeping quarters. It was not unusual to see a field of carrots, cabbage, broccoli, or corn depending on the season, that would have one hundred or more workers in it and buses or trucks of several contractors parked around the field. Some of the contractors used all or mostly all legal workers and others would have almost all illegal workers.

There were two ways to handle this kind of situation. The most obvious way was to check people in the field for their citizenship. The problem was that the illegals did not want to talk to us and, if there was any cover in the area, they would leave the field with their shirttails flapping in the wind. Sometimes we could surround a field with vehicles and arrest most or all of them, but often this was not possible.

The other method was to locate the field one day, then, early the next morning, be in position to stop the buses or trucks hauling the people to the field and check them before they dispersed into the fields. Using either method, it was often possible for the men in the Uvalde Border Patrol Station to apprehend enough persons by nine or ten-o'clock in the morning to keep us busy doing the paperwork and detention for most of the rest of the day. As part of our area control operations, we also checked the places where the labor contractors housed their personnel when we could locate them and believed that the houses contained persons illegally in the U.S.

This could sometimes be tricky. The immigration law gives an immigration officer the right to question any person as to his right to be in or remain in the U.S. However, these places were invariably on private property and usually at the rear of the residence of the person who owned them. Often, they would be surrounded by a fence high enough that the housing in question could not be seen by normal traffic through the neighborhood. No one was interested in going through the legal maneuvers to obtain a search warrant, even if there had been sufficient evidence to obtain one in most cases.

There were two ways to handle this situation when we had an idea of the neighborhood where such housing was located. One was to find one of the aliens away from the residence, such as returning from a neighborhood convenience store, and arrest him. He would know that he was about to be removed from the U.S. and would not want to leave his belongings in the residence as they would certainly be stolen. In as much as he lived there, he had a right to go into his residence and, since he was under arrest, the Border Patrolman had the right to accompany him. Once they arrived at the residence, the Border Patrolman would then exercise his right to question anyone he believed to be in the country illegally.

The other way, which was the one we used the most, was to have one man sit on the roof of one of our four wheel drive vehicles. This put him high enough to see over the fences. We would then drive the alleys of the neighborhood and if anyone could be seen outside the shelter of the dwelling, then he could be questioned. While neither method was foolproof, it did allow us to keep our area fairly clean. I worked for seventeen years in

Uvalde prior to retiring in 1987 and I do not ever remember a year when we were not the most efficient station in the Del Rio sector as to arrests per man hour worked. This held true even after we began getting trainees assigned to Uvalde straight from the academy.

The part of the Uvalde station's area that lay on the Edwards Plateau was mostly ranch land with fields in some of the river or creek bottoms. The livestock included cattle, goats, and sheep. This area was mostly rugged limestone and lots of cedar, live oak, mountain laurel, and other growth, including pecan groves in many river bottoms. It was very difficult to do effective farm and ranch checking because of the limited visibility due to the terrain and the timber. About the only time we could apprehend more than two or three aliens in a group was when we could find a group traveling together to a destination further inland or to find a construction project such as a fence building or other building project.

When I started to contact the ranchers on the plateau, some of them would ask me where Tom Hupp was. Tom was a Border Patrolman who had been stationed in Uvalde. He had left and joined the ATF (alcohol, tobacco tax, and firearms) shortly before I went to Uvalde. I never worked with him, but believe I would have liked to do so. He certainly made an impression on some tough old ranchers in that area. One of them asked me where he was and I told him that Tom had gone to ATF and was in El Paso, Texas. The rancher thought about it a minute, then said, "Well, I guess El Paso is far enough away." The man had obviously lost some of his ace hands to Tom in the past. Incidentally, Tom returned to Uvalde when he retired and built a home here. I now see him frequently and am proud to call him a friend.

★ Chapter Nineteen ★

When I reported to Uvalde, one of my favorite Border Patrol activities—sign cutting and tracking—was not being performed. From the western boundary of our area on to the north and east it was considered not suitable for sign cutting and tracking because it was limestone and rough and very difficult to work. As I became more familiar with the country, I found that many groups of aliens walked through this area in route to a more inland destination. I also found that they tended to follow well established routes such as a power line, fence line, the railroad, or parallel to a road. I started working this as time and other assignments permitted and as I became more familiar with the area my success increased to the point that later in my career, during peak months, I could and often did apprehend more than one hundred aliens per month working alone and helped apprehend additional aliens in other operations working with other men in the station.

Although, when I arrived, train check was being conducted. It was only when we could find a train sided that we would check as much of the train as we could before it moved off the siding. This was a hit-and-miss proposition and, I would submit, more miss than hit, but it did result in a few arrests from time to time. As time went on, I began to spend more time along the tracks and got a big boost in respect from the railroad after I found a place where someone had piled some rail ties and pieces of metal and other scrap on the rails in an apparent attempt to cause a derailment. I was able to use our radio to alert the railroad and get one of the detectives there before a train hit the debris.

Together, the detective and I determined who had caused the incident. He was very appreciative and, a few weeks later, the detective brought me a silver-plated belt buckle with my name engraved on it. The belt buckle is still a prized possession and I occasionally wear it. Working with him, I also learned the most effective way to check a train and, thereafter, when I spotted people on a train that I thought needed to be checked, I could almost always get the train stopped in our area so that I could check it. My ability to get the trains stopped was then sometimes better than my ability to pick my subjects to question. I once stopped a train to check a group of men that I saw on a passing train, just knowing I had a bunch (five, as I remember) of aliens to remove from the train. After getting the train stopped and approaching the car where I had seen the group of men, the first one I talked to stated that he was from "by God West Virginia." All five were hobos and there wasn't an alien in the group. I had a red face as that was the fastest express train they had and was required to maintain an average speed of 55 miles per hour between Los Angeles and St. Louis.

Mack Porter and I were compatible and liked to work together. Mack was a Texan from central Texas in the Brownwood area. At that time, we were doing a farm and ranch check in the Hill Country. There are four rivers in our area which are on the south side of the Edwards Plateau. The Sabinal, Frio, Nueces, and Leona drain a goodly portion of the plateau, forming canyons as they flow south and east to the Gulf of Mexico.

These canyons and hills were originally settled by people from Tennessee and Kentucky; some of them had not forgotten the feuds back in those states. There is still fierce competition between the various canyons and the people who live up on the divide or the top of the plateau. Mack and I were having coffee one afternoon in a cafe in Leakey which is in the Frio Canyon and is a rival of Camp Wood, which is some 20 miles to the west in Nueces Canyon.

There were two or three waitresses in the café and they were discussing a beauty pageant they were sure they would win, or at least sure their contestant would win for the district in which they lived. Mack asked one of them if they were talking about the preliminaries to the Miss America pageant and she answered yes. He then asked what made them so sure they would win. One of the girls instantly replied, "Oh, we'll win alright. Camp Wood had their pageant last week and a nanny goat won." That ranks right up there with the best put-downs I have ever heard.

Mack and I worked the Hill Country together often and swapped stories frequently. After we started getting trainees assigned to Uvalde straight from the academy, we were talking about our graduation ceremonies and I told him that Hurricane Beulah had graduated us. Mack laughed and said there had been one man in his class who probably wished something like had happened to his academy.

Mack said that, at that time, there was an Assistant or Associate Commissioner of Immigration named Clack. Commissioner Clack had come to the academy to give a speech and conduct other facets of the graduation ceremonies. One of the young trainees had consumed a couple of beers or three while waiting to attend the ceremonies. He walked somewhat unsteadily up to the commissioner and said, "Mr. Clack, is it true that your first name is Clickity?" This young man was not stationed in the same location as Mack, but Mack thought he had graduated. However, Mack would not have bet that he made probation.

The side arms issued by the patrol were issued on the basis of seniority. I had been carrying an old Colt since I didn't have enough seniority yet to get one of the newer Smith and Wessons. Then, the patrol bought a good number of new Colt Trooper models. I got one of them and had started wearing it, but after the first pistol qualifications it became apparent that the gun was somehow defective as the trigger would often not fully return after firing the gun double action. I mentioned this to Mack and told him that, after this shift, I would have to see about getting a different gun issued. He had not heard of any trouble with the guns and asked further questions. I took the loaded gun out of the holster and was holding it with the muzzle pointed to the door on my side of the vehicle (Mack was driving that morning) and while showing him what was wrong, the car went through a dip, or hit a rough place. Whatever the cause, the gun discharged.

The bullet hit the door just in front of and a little above the arm rest on my side of the car. The windows were up and, when our ears quit ringing to the point we could hear each other talk, I suggested we stop and see what damage had been done to the car. I had already looked out the window to see where the bullet might go and saw only open cedar breaks in the area. Nothing would be damaged except the car and no one could have been struck. Mack pulled over and we got out and examined the car. We were both amazed to find that the bullet had not passed through the door. I had shot the door with a full house .357 magnum but something in the door was sturdy enough to stop the bullet. Not only had it stopped the bullet, the door latch and the window still operated perfectly.

Normally, this would require a written report and possibly result in a letter of admonishment being placed in my file. No big deal. However, if any supervisor wanted to, that incident could be used as a tool to harass me. Mack and I talked it over. The only visible damage was a small hole in the door panel. We decided that if any questions arose we would not lie, as to do so would be a felony, but if no visible damage was seen by anyone, then there would be no reason for questions in the first place.

At that time, the government vehicles were kept at the home of whoever was assigned to work in that particular vehicle rather than leaving it parked on the street unattended. That afternoon after work, I went to the auto parts house, bought two of the small screws used for upholstery—the ones with chrome rings around the screw or bolt head—and popped the door panels just enough to get a hand behind them in order to put one in the hole made by the bullet. I placed the other across in the same place on the panel on the driver's side and then fastened the panels back. Once the damage was repaired, it looked just like new. Actually, it looked better than new. We probably used this vehicle for a couple more years after that and then it was moved somewhere else.

Not all gunshots in the area ended as harmlessly as the one fired into the car door. At about this time, there was an incident involving a patrolman in an adjoining area in which an alien ended up with some buckshot in him. There were so many rumors around that I never did learn for sure just how it came about, but, basically, an alien ran, a patrolman had discharged a shotgun, and the alien wound up with a hip pocket full of buckshot and ended up in a hospital. While the County Sheriff was investigating this incident, or accident, depending on which rumor you were hearing, the Sheriff was asked if it was true that the patrolman had tripped crossing the fence, causing the gun to accidentally discharge. The Sheriff, who was known to hold illegals in low esteem, was reported to have said, "If he says he fell and the gun went off, I'll believe it. Hell, I'll believe he fell twice, because I picked up two empty shells there at the fence." I never learned all the ramifications of this incident, but I do know that the patrolman went on to have a full career in the Border Patrol and is now retired.

The sheriff mentioned in the foregoing incident was well along in years and the reason that he held aliens who were illegally in the country in such low esteem was because of an incident which occurred when he was a youngster just reaching his teens. I have heard two versions of the incident and both agree that his mother was attacked and raped by an illegal alien.

The version that I heard was reportedly told by the Sheriff himself to an acquaintance when asked about it. He said that his mother was raped and killed by an illegal alien and that all the ranchers in the area told their illegal employees about this and told them to find the man who killed the woman. This was done and the man was caught and tied to a tree. Then, dry brush was piled around it. Kerosene was then poured on the brush and ignited. The other version was told to me by an acquaintance of the Sheriff who said his mother was being attacked by the alien and he killed the alien with an axe. Whichever version was correct, it happened when the sheriff was just a youngster and would have been in the 1920s or earlier. It would also account for his attitude toward illegal aliens.

We understood that the immigration service had no budget for the purpose of treating illness or injuries for aliens who were illegally in the country. I don't know where the money came from, but we were able to pay for any illness or injury incurred by an alien in our custody. We were often contacted by a hospital or other medical entity saying, in effect, that we needed to come and arrest some alien so they could collect for services rendered to this person. We were discouraged from taking custody of an alien from anyone for this purpose. We would take custody of them when they were ready for discharge and deportation, but not for the purpose of paying for their care.

I remember an instance which happened just a few miles east of Leakey on Highway 337. We were patrolling east and met a pickup with four people riding in the back. They looked like they were probably in the country illegally and I turned around on the truck, which immediately stopped, giving the people the opportunity to jump out and flee. This was a pasture with a line of trees about a hundred yards off the road. My partner talked with the driver and I went to the tree line to see what might have happened when the people got there. When I got to the tree line, I found that it marked the edge of a sheer bluff some thirty-five or forty feet deep with only a bush growing out of the side every few feet. I looked over the side where they hit the bluff and could not see any aliens or any way they could have gotten down without getting at least some injuries. I knew I certainly was not going to attempt to get down the bluff in that area.

When I got back to the truck, my partner had determined that the aliens worked for the driver of the pickup and they had pounded on the roof of the truck, demanding that he stop and let them out. My partner and I decided that if we caught any alien who had gone over that bluff, the first thing we would have to do was to have him treated for some kind of injuries. We also decided that since we now knew who their employer was and where he lived, we would let him worry about and treat the injuries they might have and we would pay him a visit at a later date.

★ Chapter Twenty ★

I enjoyed working the Hill Country. As I mentioned earlier, it was mostly populated by descendants of people who came to the area from Kentucky and Tennessee, as did my own ancestors. They were mostly rugged individuals inclined to do things their way regardless of what anyone else might think. You just never knew what you might run into, either driving the roads or walking across the hills. While I was doing work in that area, a skeleton was found in a cave near Leakey. The news media learned of it and it received a lot of coverage in one of the major area newspapers. The skeleton was examined by a noted area pathologist, who sagely opined that it had been in the cave for over a hundred years and that the hole in the cranium was caused by a bullet.

Mack Porter and I were still working that area and were drinking coffee, as we often did, with an old timer who had been a County Constable at one time and knew everyone who had lived in the Frio Canyon in the last seventy-five years. Mack mentioned the skeleton and the publicity the canyon had been getting as a result. The old timer chuckled and said he had read the paper and that they had made a poor choice when they chose the doctor to look at the skeleton. Mack asked why he said this and he said that the doctor had said the bones had been in the cave for over a hundred years, when it had actually been only fifty-four years.

Neither of us had the nerve to ask him exactly how he knew this, but I may have gotten a clue some time later. The Real County Sheriff was a friend of mine and I asked him about the case sometime later. He had heard of this and said a man had come to the county something like fifty years prior, announcing that he was a cattle detective and was there to find some stolen cattle. He had been around the area a short time before disappearing, never to be heard of again. As far as I know, the skeleton was never identified.

Most of the Border Patrolmen had never worked in law enforcement in any other venue except the Border Patrol. I had previously worked for several years as a Deputy Sheriff and was familiar with the operations and problems encountered in other agencies. I liked to work, when possible, in conjunction with both the Sheriff's Department and the Police Department in whatever local jurisdiction I happened to be working at the time. The Uvalde Police Department had hired a policeman who was very experienced and was a fine officer and we became friends. This man volunteered to be the dog handler for the Uvalde Police Department after they somehow came into possession of a pedigree bloodhound. I helped him some with the training and the dog soon did a pretty good job following a trail.

One day, I received word that a house burglary had occurred near Leakey and the Sheriff asked me to come and help with the case since he believed the burglary had been committed by aliens. A gun and some other valuables had been taken. It so happened that I was working with the dog handler at the time and he suggested that we take the dog to the scene and see if he could help. We arrived at the scene a little northeast of Leakey and I soon had the tracks the aliens had left lined out. We then put the dog out on the trail. Other officers were in contact by radio and I had a handy-talkie. The handler kept the dog on a leash and we were hard-pressed to keep up as the trail was fresh and so was the dog. The trail was soon on ground that was ninety percent rock as the burglars lined out to the east over the hills. After about 3 miles of this, I was getting ready to drop and the dog was still pulling hard.

I was saved when the officers who were staying on the road ahead of our trail saw the aliens come out of the brush and start across the road. They were arrested and I was out of breath. We were only some three hundred yards behind the burglars and would have soon overtaken them with the dog. This is the only time I ever worked a trail with a dog, but it was an exciting experience.

I have been writing about the Hill Country for some time

now, but, during this time, I had also been spending a good portion of my time in the brush and getting acquainted with the residents of the south and west part of our area. I also continued to work along the railroad, checking trains and sidings, and having considerable success in both operations.

One of the most productive areas was the Harris Ranch, a thirty- thousand acre ranch with its headquarters some twenty miles west of Uvalde. This was a working ranch that raised Santa Gertrudis cattle. I soon made friends with the ranch manager and his wife, who lived on the ranch. The ranch was also leased for hunting and there were several hunting camps scattered over the property. One of the leases was occupied during hunting season by a group of people from the medical profession and related fields.

One of these men was a technician who specialized in x-ray and other medical equipment, with whom I made a fishing trip or two to the Port Aransas area every year after I got to know him. By far the most well-known member was Dr. Robert Speegle of Garland, Texas. By the early 1970s, when I first met Dr. Speegle, he was already one of the leading big game hunters in the world. He went on to win the Weatherby award as the leading big game hunter of the world in 1979. He has hunted in many parts of the world, has countless hunting awards, and has taken just about every trophy available. He is particularly partial to mountain game wherever it may be found. I haven't seen Bob in some years as he gave up his lease in this area, but, when I last saw him, he had taken all North American big game with a rifle and was starting over, this time using a bow and arrow. He once told me that he had decided that I was just another hunter like him, only, instead of hunting big game, I was hunting men.

He often invited guests to hunt with him and, one year, he had invited a young doctor from the Houston area to come to camp for a few days. This man was a novice who had never hunted before, but he wanted to learn to rattle horns to attract a buck deer for a shot. He arrived in camp with some horns and, after some instructions, he was placed with his back against a small sage bush with a clearing in front. This was about daylight in the early morning.

When they went back to pick him up shortly before noon, he was not where they had left him and was nowhere to be seen. They began looking for him and finally located him over a mile away wandering down a ranch road without his gun, canteen, or the rattling horns. He told them that he had started rattling the horns and, after a few minutes, a buck deer had suddenly jumped over the bush from behind him and had landed almost on the young man's feet. The deer was snorting and looking for a fight, which scared the young fellow so badly that he threw his gun off his lap and jumped up running without regard as to where he was going. By the time he stopped running, he had gone so far that he could not find where he had started and had become utterly lost.

When I was a Deputy Sheriff in Knox County during the mid-60s, I had occasion to go from Benjamin to Littlefield to pick up a prisoner and return him to Benjamin. While I was in Littlefield, I met a young Highway Patrolman named Jackson. I remembered him because he had the unusual first name of Joaquin. While I was still in Benjamin, I heard he had transferred from the High Plains to Jacksboro, Texas. I never worked with him, but heard that he had been made a Texas Ranger and assigned somewhere else. I left Benjamin in 1967 and entered the U.S. Border Patrol, stationed at Eagle Pass for the next three years.

When I was transferred to the Uvalde Border Patrol station in 1970, I found that Joaquin Jackson was indeed a Texas Ranger. He was assigned to the Uvalde area and had his home there. I saw him from time to time, usually at the Sheriff's Department, but never worked with him. This changed about three years after I came to Uvalde when he called me about 3:00 a.m. one morning and asked me to go with him up into the Hill Country to assist him. He had received a report that there was a homicide at a ranch there and he had been told that aliens were involved.

I told him I would be ready in a few minutes and that he was to pick me up at home. I put on a uniform and was ready in about ten minutes. After I had waited about thirty minutes without his expected arrival at my house, I called his residence to see what had happened and found he had gone back to sleep. That made us even as each had now woken the other from a sound sleep. He finally arrived and picked me up about 4:00 a.m.

We drove up Highway 83 toward Leakey and then turned left up a Farm to Market Road near the Uvalde and Real county line. The ranch was located a few miles up the canyon. When we arrived, I realized that I knew the place and had apprehended aliens working at this place the previous year. I had apprehended a man and woman working there, processed them, and sent them back to Mexico. I remembered that the man was married and had a large family back in Mexico and that the woman who was arrested with him had been accompanying him for several years as he had been spending several months working in the U.S. every year at this ranch.

We found that the woman whom I had arrested the year before was there and that an illegal alien who had worked at the adjoining ranch up the canyon was deceased, having died of a gunshot wound. The deceased man was on a floor next to a wall. A Buck folding hunters knife was lying on his stomach and was open near his hand. I remember thinking that it looked like a carefully staged scene. The knife blade looked clean to me al-though I did not touch it. This was Joaquin's case and I was there only because there were aliens involved. The woman did not speak English, so I questioned her while Joaquin took pho-tographs of the scene, collected blood samples, and did other in-vestigative tasks.

Her story was that the deceased alien had come to visit earlier in the night and that there had been an argument between him and the man who lived with her at the ranch. This was the same man that I had handled the previous year and with whom she had been coming to the U.S. for some years. The argument had escalated into a fight and the deceased had stabbed her companion who then shot and killed the deceased. Her companion then took a utility vehicle belonging to the ranch and fled. She claimed not to know where he was going, but supposed he had intended to return to Mexico. She said she did not know how badly her companion had been injured in the fight.

While I was interviewing the woman, a vehicle came by and stopped. Joaquin talked with the driver for a few minutes and later told me that the vehicle in which the suspect had left was located a few miles down the road. The suspect had told her that he had hidden the gun and, as I remember, she claimed not to know where he had hidden it. I do not know if the gun was ever located. If it was found, I do not remember seeing it.

When Joaquin finished his examination of the scene, we took the woman and drove back to Uvalde, stopping as we passed the car in which the suspect had left the ranch. It had been angled off the highway and had suffered some damage. The suspect was nowhere to be seen. We went on to Uvalde where the woman was placed in the Uvalde County jail as an illegal alien and material witness. Believing that the shooter was either already in Mexico or attempting to reach the border, I notified both Del Rio and Eagle Pass to be on the lookout for him and to hold him for questioning if he was located.

I talked to the woman again for a few minutes a day or two later at the jail. She still maintained that her original story was true and had nothing to add to what she had already stated. That was the end of my involvement in this case. Unless Joaquin found additional evidence after I left, it was a simple case of self-defense. I do not believe either the man or woman ever returned to this ranch. I checked it from time to time thereafter and never had any indication that either of them had ever returned.

★ Chapter Twenty-One ★

After Congress passed the national 55 mph speed law in 1973, almost everyone in my area soon had citizen band radios in their cars. Many of the ranch owners and managers also installed base stations at ranch headquarters as well as all vehicles belonging to the ranch. This allowed the rancher to maintain contact with headquarters from anywhere in the ranch and also to keep abreast of operations anywhere on the ranch. A majority of vehicles traveling through the area were equipped with CB radios.

By the mid-1970s, I was spending most of my time working the railroad and ranch country in the western part of the Uvalde Station's area of responsibility. I eventually decided it would be to my advantage to add the CB radio to my other equipment.

My son, Randall, was in high school and working after school as a radio and TV technician. He installed a base station in our home and configured a mobile unit so that I could easily change it to any unit I might be working on at the time. I obtained an FCC license and call letters for the base and equipped it with a directional antenna. This allowed me to maintain contact with my home from much of the area I was working. Also, I could communicate with a number of other stations located on area ranches.

As to the mobile unit, I needed a "handle" if I was to make the best use of it in the field. Sylvia suggested that "Trailblazer" would be a great handle. That suited me, so "Trailblazer" it was. I was surprised at the number of people driving through the area who would see the antenna on my vehicle and report aliens they had seen back down the road somewhere. The CB radio was entertaining and allowed me to apprehend many aliens I would have otherwise missed.

I had learned the brush country in our area to the point where I could find a fresh trail where aliens had passed and usually know which of the well-used routes they would follow as they traveled. I was working alone much of the time, but could usually get a Border Patrol aircraft. I did not call for a plane unless the sign was fresh and we had a good chance of making apprehensions. Since it was productive, the pilots were willing to come almost any time. I was also checking many of the passing trains and learned that many groups of aliens would walk to a siding in our area and make camp while waiting for a train to side, then would get on the sided train and ride on toward San Antonio.

By this time, I was parking my vehicle where it could not be seen from the camping places and walking out the draws and live oak groves where the most used camping places were located. The Border Patrol pilots had learned that the camped aliens would almost always build a fire at night, so they flew the railroad before daylight, locating fires. They would not circle, but would note the location of the fires and call the station responsible for the area. When the agents approached the area, the pilot would return and assist with the arrests. Alien traffic had increased considerably and the Uvalde Station was apprehending more and more aliens. The agents assigned to this station were all experienced men who knew what needed to be done and how to do it.

About this time, the Commissioner of Immigration, who had been appointed by either Nixon or Ford, paid a visit to California and decided to send some help from other parts of the border upon being told what dire straits the Border Patrol personnel in that area were in because of the great number of aliens.

It did not matter who was President. There always seemed to be a Commissioner that I could not believe had good qualifications to handle the Immigration and Naturalization Service. Even after I retired, it didn't look like it was getting better. George H. W. Bush appointed a lawyer from St. Louis, Missouri. I heard he was a political appointee who, when he was appointed Commissioner, became an expert on all things having to do with Mexico and immigration affairs by going to his local college in St. Louis and talking with the professors who taught Spanish at the university. I also heard that when he entered the first Border Patrol office the first question he asked was, "What was that man doing wearing a gun?" (He was referring to one of the officers in the office.)

I am not reporting these things as facts. I am just reporting what I heard from officers who were in the patrol at the time. If this was true, it would not be surprising to me. Another President, I believe it was Carter, appointed a man who was controller of Houston, Texas, as Commissioner. I don't know what qualified this man to be Commissioner. Even today, it has not changed much. Although the Border Patrol is now part of the Department of Homeland Security, the Secretary recently issued an advisory on terrorism that included all returning veterans and such right-wing extremists as people who think abortion is morally wrong.

Whatever the Commissioner's thinking was, we were required to send a certain number of men from this region to Southern California. The detail was for one month periods, and I and one other man from Uvalde went with the first wave. We found that the guys in California did indeed need help. They were almost as busy there as we had been back home. This was a very enjoyable trip for me. I traveled to California in my own car. I reported in at the Chula Vista Sector and I was assigned to the Temecula station.

Temecula was a small town with few places to stay. We stayed in motels in nearby Fallbrook, a beautiful town in a resort area in the coastal mountains. This was June and the nights were chilly with the days just about perfect. As soon as we got settled in, some of us (including me) sent for our wives to join us. My wife and daughter came with the other man's wife and spent the rest of the time with us. I stayed an extra week just to give them more time to do things like visit Universal City, the Hearst Castle, Palomar Observatory, and other points of interest. Our detail in California was successful. When I saw the numbers of arrests for our stay there, I noticed that we had apprehended just about the same number of people we were apprehending at home before we left.

California had recently enacted a law restricting the amount of money that a tow truck operator could charge for towing and storage. It was either two or three hundred dollars. Any money above that amount was confiscated by the state. However, the tow truck operator was given the privilege of selling the vehicles for the state. The salvage yard operator in Fallbrook did not think that was fair and, since the Border Patrol operation was keeping his yard full of cars, many of which were to be sold for storage, he needed space and offered to sell some of them for the amount he was allowed to keep. I bought a nice Pontiac and towed it back to Texas behind my car.

We came back east via I-40 and stopped by the south rim of the Grand Canyon as we went through Arizona. All in all, it was the best, most enjoyable detail of my twenty years in the Border Patrol. I called the senior agent for whom I had worked at Temecula and told him I would volunteer for the August detail if he could get me transferred to Temecula from Chula Vista where the August detail was scheduled to go. The senior liked my work and readily agreed to get me back to Temecula as I already knew the operation there. He soon called me back and said the personnel officer in Chula Vista already had the list of men scheduled to report there and would not change it. Mack Porter was due to perform the next month-long detail from our station and I told him I had tried, but he would have to take his turn after all. I had learned enough about Chula Vista when I was there in June to know that I didn't want to go there for a month. Mack told me when he got back to Uvalde that they had called him LaMascus for the entire time he was there. I had told him before he left to give the personnel officer a suggestion from me concerning what he could do with the personnel list he was so proud of.

I did not mention this when I wrote about the academy, but this seems like a good time to do so since I am already in California. My academy was one man short. George Azrak had entered on duty at the Temecula station about the same time I had gone to Eagle Pass and was scheduled to be in the same academy. Just before he was to report to the academy, he was working a two-man traffic check at a point known as Oak Grove. It was located about twenty miles out of Temecula at the base of the mountain where the Palomar Observatory is located. His partner was Theodore Newton, who was himself just off probation, having only about one year in the patrol. They were working a night shift and stopped a hearse with two occupants who were both U. S. citizens. They had released it, but stopped it again and found that it contained several hundred pounds of marijuana. The load was being followed by another vehicle with two occupants who in some way managed to stop behind the first vehicle and take both patrolmen by surprise and disarm them. They were taken to an abandoned cabin in the area, handcuffed to a stove in the cabin, and later killed with one of their own guns.

The killers were caught and convicted. I believe that incident was supposed to have resulted in a change of official Border Patrol policy so that there would be no more two-man points, but I worked that same checkpoint often while I was in California and was routinely assigned to work a two-man point. At least, I don't remember there being a third man present when I worked that point. I was routinely assigned to work two-man points in both Eagle Pass and Uvalde. I also worked the point on I-15 just out of Temecula and there were always several men on that point. I go through checkpoints in the Uvalde area from time to time now and have not seen a two-man point in years. I hope the Patrol has discontinued all two-man points.

I was on a weeklong detail in the San Antonio and Austin areas a few months after the California experience. We were checking construction sites and businesses which were known to use a lot of illegal employees. We would take a bus and several units and, by noon, or shortly thereafter, would usually have the bus and the various units full of prisoners and be ready to return to San Antonio for processing the rest of the day. One of the men I worked with on that detail was from Laredo and often did undercover work, including working with informants on the Mexican side of the border in Nuevo Laredo. He told me he sat at a table in one of the bars there and listened as several men whom he knew were smugglers of both aliens and narcotics talked about ambushing and taking out an entire checkpoint on the American side. He thought that the only reason they had not already made an attempt to do so was because they had not been able to devise a plan that would assure them a good chance of making an escape back to Mexico.

★ Chapter Twenty-Two ★

Just south of the escarpment marking the southern edge of the Edwards Plateau, FM 2690 runs from Highway 83 ten miles north of Uvalde east to Highway 127. This road crosses both the Frio River and the Dry Frio River which are some four or five miles apart at this point. There are low water crossings at both rivers on FM 2690. I was working in this area one day when I saw a group of four people, whom I believed to be aliens, leave an abandoned farm house and go into rough country moving northeast toward Utopia. I called to see if anyone was close and found that Mack Porter was in the general area. I told him what I had seen and I would be out of my vehicle with a handy-talkie, trying to apprehend these four aliens. I told him I could use some help because it might take some time and distance for me to catch up to them.

Mack started that way and I left my vehicle to follow the trail the aliens had used as they left the farm house. It took me close to an hour and something like three miles to finally catch up to and capture the aliens. Mack then drove his vehicle as close as he could to my location and I walked with the prisoners to his vehicle. He then took me back to my vehicle and we started driving to the office to process them as it was late in the day and time to quit work and go home. When we came to the Dry Frio River, we found it was a torrent and much too deep to cross. It had been dry when we had crossed earlier. I had noticed some clouds in the hills earlier in the day, but I had no idea it had rained that much.

This development was an inconvenience because it meant that we would have to go back east to Highway 127 and then down FM 1049 to Knippa in order to get back to Uvalde. We drove east on FM 2690 until we got to the point where it crossed the main

Frio River and discovered that this river was also up and running over the road as deep or deeper than had been the Dry Frio. We were trapped between the rivers which were both not only too deep to drive across, they were also too deep and swift to attempt to cross by wading, especially with four prisoners—two of whom could not swim.

To walk out would be a walk of over ten miles of rough country, much of which would have been during hours of darkness since it was late in the day. We decided to spend the night. The aliens had very little food for their dinner, but ate what they would have eaten had they not been apprehended. Mack had no emergency rations with him and I had only a can of Vienna sausage and some crackers, which I shared with him. We went to the abandoned farm house and found a room where we would be dry. We handcuffed the prisoners together and took turns guarding them until the next morning when we called and got a pilot to bring the four seat Cessna aircraft to come for us. He landed on the road, took Mack and two prisoners to the airport, then came back and got me and the other two prisoners. Mack told me that the next time I called for help to be sure to remind him to bring lunch and a pillow. It was about a week before the water went down enough that we could get our vehicles back across the river.

I soon got back into the normal routine after returning from California. Our alien traffic was increasing and there was enough to keep me busy along the railroad and through the ranches in the western part of our area. I had gotten to know all the ranchers and ranch managers in that area and I got along well with them. Two of the most productive areas were the Cline and the Mines area. The area known as the Mines was a few miles south of U.S. Highway 90 and some 15 miles west from Uvalde. There are two mining operations which mine rock asphalt, which is used for paving the surface of roads and are the largest rock asphalt mines in the world. The Texas Highway Department has a laboratory nearby to monitor the quality of the material the State of Texas buys.

Cline is a community where a Calvary post protected area settlers in frontier times and protected the road from San Antonio to Del Rio. It is located on Highway 90 about 20 miles west of Uvalde and is now largely abandoned, having only three or four houses. The headquarters of the Harris ranch was nearby. I got along well with the manager there and often stopped by for coffee. There were several bushes of pepper growing around the house and the manager's wife had picked a pint jar full of the peppers to make them into a powder. These were little chilepetin peppers, which are round, not much larger than a BB, and very hot. They are red when mature. She baked them in the oven until they were completely dry. I took them home, and ran them in my blender until they were powder and looked just like the powdered Cayenne that can be found in the grocery stores. I took them back and she put the powder in a little jar on the kitchen table.

I stopped by for coffee one morning and they had several visitors, one of whom was a shrimp boat Captain from the Corpus Christi area. Another was their son who was visiting from Ocala, Florida, where he was a well-known trainer of thoroughbred race horses. Someone was making small tortillas and set a plate of these on the table as the shrimper sat down. He took one, and as he buttered the tortilla, the son slid the jar of pepper toward his plate and said, "Here is a little seasoning." After spreading the butter on the tortilla the shrimper took a teaspoon and dipped it in the powdered pepper, carefully leveled it in the spoon with a knife, then sprinkled it on the tortilla, rolled the tortilla up, and took about half the tortilla with the first bite. As he bit down, I could see him chewing slower and slower as sweat popped out of his forehead and he began stifling the urge to cough. It was evident that he was having difficulty eating and trying to hide it. The son was in an adjoining room and I could see him convulsing with laughter. Finally, someone handed the poor fellow a glass of water and not a minute too soon. I don't know if the Captain ever knew why the pepper he thought was cayenne was so hot.

The Southern Pacific Railroad runs along part of the southern boundary of the Harris ranch while a ranch road paralleled the railroad a short distance inside the ranch. This was a very productive area for alien arrests as this was also a siding for the railroad known as the Obi siding. There were two windmills in this area where aliens who were waiting for a train to stop could get water. One of the windmills was on a rise and could be seen from a similar high point along Highway 90, which paralleled the railroad one-half mile distant. I would stop on Highway 90 and, using my binoculars, look around the windmill on the rise and see aliens passing or getting water from this windmill. I could then call for a plane which would usually work in the Brackettville area and get the pilot to spot the aliens for me or hold them hidden until I could get there because I had to drive two miles on the highway to the ranch entrance, then back on the ranch road.

On one particular morning, I stopped on Highway 90 and, upon scanning the area, I could see a group of seven going up the rise to the windmill. One of the men wore a bright red shirt. I called for the airplane and as I left to get to the ranch road, they walked away from the windmill. The plane got to the area along the siding before I could get there and was looking the area over. I told him to look for a bright red shirt. When looking for aliens hidden in the brush, the pilot usually could not see a whole person, but would see a small spot of color, which might be the only thing visible even though several men could be hidden.

By the time I got my vehicle over the road inside the ranch, the pilot had spotted aliens hidden in a live oak mott. I drove to them, but none of them was wearing a red shirt. I asked who had the red shirt thinking he might have changed, but no one had a red shirt. I told the pilot that he had caught the wrong bunch and to keep trying. He laughed and started looking over the area again. He found another group, but, on arriving where they were hidden, I found no red shirt in that bunch either. I assured the pilot that I had seen a red shirt and wanted to see it again. He started looking again and I called by radio to get another unit for help since I had more people than I could haul.

I guarded the ones I had in custody and the pilot kept searching. Just before the other unit got to us, the pilot said he could see red in a mott across the railroad from where I was holding the others. He got on his loud speaker, talked them into surrendering, and walked them the hundred yards or so where I was holding the others. By the time the other units arrived, I was holding over twenty prisoners that we had apprehended in just thirty minutes. Every one of them was waiting for a train to take the siding so they could ride on toward San Antonio.

Since I have mentioned one of our pilots, I will talk some more about them. By the 1980's, we were using some helicopters and I liked to fly as observer in them when the opportunity arose. Most of the time, we were working with a pilot who was flying a Super Cub. At that time, all the Border Patrol pilots were Border Patrolmen who had worked on the ground and were well-acquainted with ground operations as well as being superb pilots. Our vehicles had numbers painted on top in order for the pilot to know which vehicle they were talking to when working with more than one unit in the field. Some of the pilots delighted in finding a man or team working alone in the field. The unit would have no idea there was an aircraft in the area. The pilot would gain some altitude and then dive toward the unsuspecting man or men in the vehicle, keeping the motor throttled back until they were just above the target vehicle. The pilot would then give the plane full power and pull up about twenty feet above the unit with a teeth-rattling roar. Regardless of how many times a person had experienced this, it would always scare one half to death for a moment.

I was working one day in the Cline area and was stopped by a motorist on Highway 90 who reported that he had passed two men five miles to the west that were walking along the roadway and appeared to possibly be from Mexico. I drove to check it out and, upon arriving in the area, stopped short of the top of a hill and walked forward to look across the valley ahead. I could see the men roughly one and a half miles ahead. Knowing that if I tried to drive to them they would recognize the Border Patrol vehicle and probably hit the brush, making it difficult or impossible for me to apprehend them, I called for a plane which I could hear on the radio and was working nearby.

As the pilot approached, I explained the situation. He came in above the roadway from behind the walkers. He had some altitude and, when I could see him getting near the men, I drove forward and topped the hill some one mile ahead of the men. They spotted my vehicle and headed for the fence just as the pilot pulled up right over their heads and gave the plane full throttle. This scared the guys so badly I had to go to the tree they were hidden under and literally drag them out. By now, the plane was flying in lazy circles around us, but the men were so terrified they were afraid to stand up straight.

Not long after the incident, Mack Porter had to take a vehicle to Del Rio for service of some kind and I took another vehicle to bring him back, as he was to leave his there for the service work. On the way back, I entered the Harris Ranch, intending to drive through the ranch and exit on another road. I wanted to check the Obi siding area on the way through. We had just turned down parallel to the railroad when we saw a group of aliens walking down the road ahead of us. By driving slowly and keeping the vehicle from making much noise, I was able to get close before one of them looked back, saw us, and ran. Mack caught one of them just as he reached the fence between the ranch and the railroad. He snapped one cuff on a wrist, slapped the fence with the other, and immediately pursued another nearby alien.

I had driven ahead of them in the vehicle, and, together, we managed to get all or most of the others in custody within the next 20 to 30 minutes. We then went back to get the one Mack parked on the fence. The road was some fifty yards from the fence, and I waited in the vehicle while Mack walked down to get the man. When they came back, they were laughing and I heard the alien tell Mack he was afraid we would forget where we had left him. Mack said he noticed the man standing in an unusual way as he got close, and discovered the ranch had recently hooked a fence charger to the top wire of the fence. The alien was standing, holding the cuff on the fence so it was clear of the wire. No damage was done to the alien, but it didn't take him long to decide to hold the cuff clear of the wire.

Before they ran, I had noticed as we got close that one of the men seemed to be dragging something and, as we went back down the road, I saw that it was a very large rattlesnake. They had killed the snake before we found them and were intending to clean and cook it for a meal after they had made camp. As I drove away, I wondered what the Customs Inspector I worked with on Operation Intercept in Eagle Pass would have done if he had seen that huge snake.

★ Chapter Twenty-Three ★

The day arrived when the Patrol Agent in Charge of the Uvalde station reached mandatory retirement age. He and I had our differences, but we worked around them and managed to work together in the most efficient station in the sector. No new supervisor had been appointed at the time of his retirement.

The senior officers of the station rotated as Acting Patrol Agent in Charge. The station continued to run efficiently and was still the best in the sector. This arrangement lasted several months, possibly a year, then a man transferred from the lower Rio Grande valley and was station supervisor for a couple of years. His tenure saw the alien traffic continue to increase.

The Southern Pacific Railroad hauled a lot of new vehicles from the west coast eastward. Hobos and aliens (mostly aliens) found ways to not only get in the car carriers, but to break into the vehicles. They were using radios, heaters, and in general, doing a lot of damage. The trains were being checked in some places near the border, but the railroad veered away from the border, leaving Del Rio. There were still sidings where the aliens could walk and wait for a train to side. Our area was the most distant from where that would happen, and we began to work in conjunction with the railroad detectives in organized train check operations.

There were access roads along each side of the railroad at Knippa, Texas, which is in the Uvalde area of responsibility. The Knippa siding was chosen as the site to check all eastbound trains for several consecutive days at a time. A helicopter would be assigned to Uvalde, equipped with a very strong battery of spotlights for nighttime operations. This was a highly successful operation and was continuing at the time I retired. There were times when more than one hundred aliens could be found on a single eastbound train. Except in aggravated cases, no criminal charges were being filed against the illegal aliens apprehended in these operations. They were processed the same day they were apprehended and returned to Mexico at either Del Rio or Eagle Pass. There were a few times when we apprehended the same group of people as often as three consecutive nights.

Theft of electronic equipment was another type of crime dogging the railroad detectives at that time. The thieves were believed to have an accomplice among the railroad employees since the piggybacks (trailers with aluminum containers, pulled by trucks) were being broken into as the trains were traveling east. Inside the containers were expensive electronic equipment. The damaged containers with the missing equipment were arriving in San Antonio after they had been checked and found OK further west. These people were not being apprehended in the regular train check operations.

I found a railroad bridge in the Cline area where the railroad was just next to Highway 90, where a vehicle could be driven under either the highway or the railroad bridge. I found two trails where large, heavy sacks had been dragged from the rails, down the embankment, and under the bridge where there were fresh tire tracks. The drag marks ended at the tracks and I believed the sacks had been loaded into the vehicle. I concluded that this was how the electronics thieves were getting the goods off the trains. I gave the information to the railroad detectives and they took it from there.

I was later informed that a case had been made involving a railroad employee somewhere to the west (I believe it was Sanderson) who was furnishing information to the ring of thieves concerning which containers contained the valuable cargos. The thieves would put a man or two on the rail car and they would break the seals on the container. While the train was moving, they would load up sacks with the valuables while the other members of the gang paralleled the train on Highway 90. When the train sided or stopped, the sacks were taken off and loaded into the vehicle. This ring was broken up. I am sure people were prosecuted but did not hear anything else about this operation.

From time to time, we were assigned to operate a checkpoint some 23 miles west of Uvalde near a railroad overpass. This operation was intermittent back then and would be operated for several days, then become inactive again. We never knew what would come through this point. Although Highway 90 left the border area after passing Del Rio going east, it began at Los Angeles. When working that particular point, we got a sample of everything.

A favorite thing for many aliens was to steal a bike after crossing the river and ride it to his destination. I saw a likely suspect come over the overpass and approach the point one day. Upon his stopping at the point, I asked him in my best Spanish what his nationality was and where he was going. He did not answer, but started digging in his saddlebags and handed me documentation showing that he was from Yokohama, Japan, and had entered at Los Angeles. He was going to Miami, Florida. He did not speak a word of English. I waved him on and wished him luck, admiring his courage.

I was not on the point at the time, but was told of an occurrence which still brings a smile when I think of it. It was during the springtime and there had been some rain. There were flowers everywhere including blue bonnets and acres of little yellow flowers which no one knew the name of. The story was that a car bearing New Jersey license plates stopped at the point and a lady leaned out the window and asked the Patrolman if he knew what the name was for those little yellow flowers that she was seeing along the road. The quick thinking young fellow had no more idea what the name for the flowers was than the rest of us did, but he did know what "yellow flowers" meant in Spanish.

He immediately said, "Yes, ma'am, those are called flores amarillas." The lady thanked him profusely and went on her way thrilled that she now knew the correct name for those little yellow flowers.

In 1979, I was checking a train with Mack Porter at the siding in Uvalde, when I slipped and fell on the steps of a freight car and injured my back. This kept getting worse until I was forced to have surgery to repair a damaged disc in my lower back in early 1980. The surgeon repaired two ruptured discs and the recuperation took several months. The fact that no light duty was available in the Uvalde station kept me inactive for most of the year. I finally persuaded my doctor to release me back to duty shortly before Reagan took office as President.

I started spending more time in the Hill Country. The alien traffic had gotten worse and the Sheriff of Real County had started calling on all the reports he was getting, enough to keep one man well occupied. The Sheriff of Real County at that time was Buck Miller. He and I had always gotten along and worked well together even though we were in different agencies. When not occupied in Real County, there was no shortage of things to do.

Alien traffic was heavy just about anywhere I looked. Garner State Park is located off Highway 83 ten miles south of Leakey in Uvalde, County. The park is on the beautiful Frio River and is a very popular recreation area which would have thousands of people present on almost any weekend. I would often take one of the maxi vans and go to the intersection of roads coming into 83 headed toward the park. I talked to incoming people from the San Antonio and Austin areas and ask them what route they had followed and if they had seen any groups of people walking the roads. Almost any morning I could locate from one to several groups of aliens traveling through the area and succeed in apprehending them. They would think they had already gotten by all the Border Patrol activity and my vehicle would not be recognized as a government vehicle until I had already stopped and was in their midst. The best day I can remember was the day I got the area behind the security screen so full I had to start putting the prisoners in front with me. When I unloaded back at the office, there were 32 prisoners in the van.

We tend to think of the illegal alien as coming to the U.S., finding a job, sending money back to his family in Mexico, or some other country, and generally being an industrious addition to the labor force. There are exceptions to this picture.

In the early 1980s, I began to notice a particular young fellow who I would see occasionally walking down a street in Uvalde. He always had a book under his arm. He usually had a white dress shirt, a tie, and, depending on the weather, a coat. Since he seemed to frequent a particular neighborhood, I asked the owner of the neighborhood grocery store if he knew this fellow. He said he did not know a name, but the guy came occasionally for small purchases. The man was staying at a church down the street, which was headquarters for a religious sect, and had been seen around the neighborhood for the past couple of months. The grocer said he spoke almost no English and he was of the opinion that the minister in charge of the church was being charitable and taking care of this fellow while trying to convert him to his faith. He thought that the clothes he wore and the money he spent were being furnished by the church, or that the church or someone connected with the church had arranged to get him on some public assistance program. He did not seem to be employed and was never seen doing any work.

Not long after I talked to the grocer, I noticed a bus come in from San Antonio and let this fellow off a couple of blocks short of the bus station. He was dressed in slacks, shirt, and tie. He carried a jacket over his shoulder. He also carried the book under his arm. He was walking toward the church which was several blocks away. I decided to check him out. I waited until he was past the downtown traffic, then pulled up ahead of him, got out of the vehicle, and waited until he approached. I asked about his citizenship and immigration status and learned he was a citizen of Mexico and had no immigration documents. I then asked where he worked. He said he was looking for Jesus. That opening was so good I just could not pass it up. I guess you could say the Devil made me do it.

I informed him that this was his lucky day. I said that I happened to know that Jesus was in Piedras Negras, Mexico, that day and that I had a bus that was going to the Port of Entry there at about four o'clock that afternoon. I assured him I would see that he had a seat on the bus and that he should have no trouble finding Jesus when he got to Piedras Negras. In effect, I took him off the gravy train and put him on the immigration bus. I never saw him again.

★ Chapter Twenty-Four ★

While Buck Miller was Sheriff of Real County, there was a fire at a house in Camp Wood, which is in Real County. There was an elderly woman living in the house. She had been badly burned and was deceased when the fire department put the fire out and the house could be entered. I first heard about this when the Sheriff asked me about autopsies. He had talked to the funeral director who conducted the funeral and said he had been told that the body was so badly burned that an autopsy would not be helpful. I never saw the death certificate but a Justice of the Peace acting as Coroner must have found the death accidental.

Whatever had preceded, when the Sheriff asked about autopsies I remembered the homicide seminar in Austin where the Coroner of Harris County had shown numerous films of autopsies he had performed and the surprising things they had revealed. It seemed that younger relatives of the deceased woman had been working with and associating with a young man from Mexico. Shortly after the fire, the relatives had seen the fellow in possession of an item or items that they believed had come from the house of the deceased woman. They knew he had been smoking marijuana the evening of the fire and suspected that he had murdered the woman and caused the fire. They had communicated their suspicions to the Sheriff.

I assured Buck that an autopsy would almost certainly show if the woman was alive or deceased prior to the fire and probably the cause of death if it was a homicide. Since the suspect was an alien and suspected to be illegally in the U.S., he asked if I would assist with the case if an autopsy proved it to be a homicide. I agreed and he arranged for the disinterment and an autopsy.

It must have been some two weeks or so later when I received word by radio that Buck wanted me to come by the Sheriff's office in Leakey. When I arrived, I found that he had received the autopsy report and that it had indeed been a homicide. Not only was she deceased before the fire, there was a sizable tear in the wall of the vagina indicating sexual trauma after the death had occurred. Buck was ready to make an arrest in the case.

I went with him and acted as translator when the arrest was made and Miranda warning was given. We took the defendant from Camp Wood back to Leakey where I was asked to question the man and act as translator for the Sheriff. I believe that while we were doing that, the subject's residence was searched, and items believed to have belonged to the deceased were found and identified by her relatives. At first, he denied having anything to do with a burglary or death, but after being told of the search of his residence and the results, he confessed that he had been high after smoking marijuana and had smothered the woman with a pillow. After taking the money and items, he had set the fire that he had wrongly believed would destroy the evidence of murder. The vaginal tearing was inflicted after death by use of a pair of binoculars which was also found in his residence.

I took a written statement from him for the Sheriff. We now had a capital murder case that I believed would stand judicial scrutiny. I was never called to testify in this case, but remember being told he had made a plea bargain for 99 years in prison to avoid a trial for capital murder. Buck Miller is now Sheriff of Menard County and lives in Menard, Texas. He was and is a fine officer and Menard County is fortunate to have him as their Sheriff.

During this period of time, the Hill Country population was increasing by leaps and bounds. Subdivisions and communities of acreages were springing up in various places and the area around Leakey was no exception. Many were retirement residences, but there were also vacation cabins and others built by people who just wanted to live in a place with beautiful surroundings. Some people thought the remote area would be a good area for a meth lab and an occasional case would now be made in that area. When I patrolled in that part of our territory, I kept my eyes open for anything. My primary responsibility was for immigration and naturalization violations, but my past experience in other venues of law enforcement caused me to recognize violations that I might have otherwise overlooked.

In one particular situation, I noticed quite a bit of activity in the Leakey area. A recreational vehicle had been parked and a foundation was being prepared. Some of the acreage was being cleared by aliens who I later apprehended. I located the owner of the property who was living in the recreation vehicle and directing the building and clearing. I allowed the aliens to collect their wages and processed them as normal. They had been sleeping in a shack on the back of the property. A few weeks later, I saw the clearing was again being done and apprehended another group of aliens. By this time, the building of a dwelling was well underway and, again, I allowed the aliens to collect their wages. My contact with the owner and the people he was associated with had now caused me to believe there was something peculiar about this whole operation.

This time, I took license numbers of vehicles and ran them. They were all out of state and the results only deepened the mystery. None were registered to the owner of the property. I then checked with the Sheriff to see what he knew about these new residents of the county. He had only met the man briefly one time and knew very little except that he had flown in and out of the local airport in a very expensive airplane a few times. I told him of my suspicions, what I knew of him, and the people he had at the property.

The Sheriff decided to try to find out who he was and made it a point to get a good look at him the next time he came to town. He then contacted a narcotics team and they brought pictures among other evidence. They handed the Sheriff picture after picture of possible suspects when they came to one and tossed it aside, saying it would not be this one because he was dead. The Sheriff saw the picture face up as it slid across the desk and said, "Let me see that." It was his man. He had disappeared the year before (as far as the narcotics team knew) and believed to have died when a Mexican plane crashed. According to what the Sheriff told me, the man was considered by the narcotics team to be a mystery, but of interest. I had no further dealings with this situation and left it, knowing that, I had at least brought the fellow back from the dead.

It was about this time in my career that I experienced one of the shortest high-speed chases of my career as part of a smuggling case. I was leaving Uvalde one day, driving along the road, which was parallel to the railroad, and made a curve toward Highway 90. I was just a short distance beyond the curve when I met a car that I could see had the back seat full of people who were ducked down below the level of the window. I was driving a four wheel drive utility vehicle which was tall enough to let me look down through the windows. I turned around on the car as it went around the curve and immediately called on the radio to see if there was a unit available to block the road at Uvalde as I knew I could not catch up before town, which was only some two miles away. Before I could round the curve and see up the road, the car was topping a hill halfway to town. He had seen me brake to turn and was really "hauling it." I had lucked out.

James Banks, who had transferred from Eagle Pass at the same time I had, was crossing the railroad from the north and was in perfect position. James set as close to a perfect one man block as there is. He turned his vehicle crossways over half of the two lane road so the Border Patrol markings would be clearly visible. He then stood in the middle of what road was left, pulled his gun, let the approaching driver see it by holding it up, then it leveled it at the oncoming car. As I topped the hill a mile behind the car, I saw smoke start to boil up around it as the driver stood on the brakes in a desperate attempt to stop before the officer began shooting. He got it shut down just as he came up to James' location. I pulled up and stopped, and as I walked by the car, I not only could smell the smoke, but I could also feel the heat from the brakes and wheels as I walked by. That was a very fast vehicle and the driver was not the owner. The owner later got the car back and told the wrecker service owner that he had spent a lot of money making the car fast.

★ Chapter Twenty-Five ★

The Uvalde station was one where the men were all experienced, knew what to do, how to do it, could make a supervisor look good if given a little encouragement, and left to do their jobs. This happened to the supervisor who had come from the lower Rio Grande Valley and he took a promotion and was replaced by a patrolman who was promoted from another station in the sector to be Patrol Agent in Charge of the Uvalde station. This man was well-liked, had a good reputation in the sector, but I had never met him.

His name was Sammie Stewart. He was from the central Texas area. At that time, our office was in a building across from the Uvalde Memorial Hospital and had enough fenced space behind it to park our vehicles and also a few vehicles that had been seized after being used in illegally transporting aliens in the country or other classes of contraband. These vehicles would be driven to sector headquarters from time to time. When Sammie arrived, it was time to take one of the seized cars to Del Rio for its final disposition.

I remembered this car. It had been seized a couple of months ago. The Uvalde Police Department had stopped the car and, after determining that it contained illegal aliens, had called our office and a team of Border Patrolmen had responded. By the time I got to work the next morning, the case had been processed and all persons involved had been transported to Del Rio. A few days later, we learned that the person driving the car had a warrant, or was wanted, in Chicago for some kind of narcotics violation. Nothing came of this because the case had already been disposed and the subject had either been released or returned to Mexico.

The morning after the car was seized, I was asked to make sure it was transferred from the open parking lot behind the county jail where it had been left after the city had stopped it the night before to the parking lot behind our office. The keys were in the Sheriff's office. I went into the Sheriff's office to get the keys and call for one of our units to help me move the car to our office. When I got in the Sheriff's office, I found the Chief of Police in the office and he was about ready to leave to go to his office. I asked if he would have time to drive the seized car to our office and he readily agreed. I was given the keys and told the car had been searched the night before by the city and Border Patrol officers who had made the case. I gave the keys to the Chief and followed him to our office where we left the car. I then took him to his office.

It was Sammie's first day as Patrol Agent in Charge. He came by the office to pick up some papers and was going to sector headquarters for orientation or paperwork involving his new job. I was going to drive the seized vehicle to Del Rio and ride back with the new Patrol Agent in Charge. He was getting his things together in preparation to go. I took the keys to the vehicle and went to the parking lot, unlocked it, and began to get it ready to go. It had not been started in about two months. I raised the hood, checked the water and, as I reached for the oil dipstick, I noticed an olive drab sack stuffed in behind the wheel well on the driver's side of the car. I looked in the duffle bag and could see that it contained some 10 to 15 pounds of what was almost certainly marijuana tightly wrapped in clear plastic.

I thought about the case as I finished checking the oil and got the car started. I then went inside and told Sammie what I had found. He thought about it a minute, then asked me what I thought. I gave him a rundown on the case. No defendant, no chain of evidence. Sector might get their bowels in an uproar and want to discipline the guys who made the case for not properly searching the car, but all we had was a bunch of marijuana, which could cause a headache.

I told him if it were up to me, I would build a bonfire, burn the stuff, and forget I ever saw it. He kept getting ready, gathering up papers and putting them in a briefcase. When he was ready, he picked up the keys to his vehicle, looked at me and said, "Where are we going to build this bonfire?"

I knew right then we had a winner and time proved that to be one hundred percent correct. It was a cool winter morning and there was a good breeze from the southeast. We left Highway 90 and drove to a nearby railroad siding where we burned the weed. We had a good laugh and agreed that there were probably a bunch of happy coyotes and jack rabbits in the pasture. Since then, I have thought of that as our ten thousand dollar bonfire.

Not long after Sammie became Patrol Agent in Charge of the Uvalde station, he made another good decision. My son, David, completed probation in the Brackettville station a few months before and wanted to transfer back to Uvalde, where he had lived prior to entering the patrol. His wife was employed in Uvalde and they had already moved back from Brackettville after he finished probation. He was driving to work .already and the transfer would be no expense to the government and would involve only the paperwork.

This transfer was not prohibited by any rule or regulation, but many supervisors were hesitant to station a father and son in the same station. I was not involved in any discussion about this, but I understood when Sammie brought it up, the Chief Patrol Agent said, "That don't blow my skirts up. If the man wants to go to Uvalde, then let's send him to Uvalde." David had a good record, finished in the same place in his class at the academy as I had, and had all the qualities to make a top hand. The Uvalde station had the men who could give him the guidance and experience to make him a finished officer.

About the same time, we received the first trainees that had ever been assigned to the Uvalde station directly from the Academy. It had been the policy to station all new patrolmen on the Mexican border for the first year. The Uvalde station was not responsible for any of the river crossings as our closest area of responsibility was thirty miles from the Rio Grande. The Uvalde station was considered a back-up station. We never had an opportunity to apprehend anyone who had not already passed through someone else's area of responsibility. When a man reports to a Border Patrol station from the Academy, the only thing we could be sure about was that he was no dummy. All the tests during the hiring process and the academy had assured that. The only way to tell what kind of officer he was going to be was to put him through the ringer of everyday duties, doing the various kinds of work done in the station and see how he stood up. By the time a man had passed the tests and spent the time and money involved, he already had quite an investment in the job and the Border Patrol had a considerable investment in him.

It was my opinion that our job as journeymen officers working with a trainee was not to harass or just look for something in order to criticize, but to instruct, encourage, and advise so that a trainee could reach his full potential. That is not to say a trainee would not be the butt of a few jokes or good-natured teasing (after all, a group of southwesterners could not be expected to sit at a table drinking coffee with a good natured young fellow from Rhode Island without teaching him things like: y'all is not a small boat, but means all of you, or that war was what you put around the pasture to keep the cows from straying), but nothing detrimental to his becoming the best he could. I know Sammie felt the same way, having heard him say basically the same thing when some question arose about the training of these men.

★ Chapter Twenty-Six ★

Well, the trainees arrived and I was impressed. A giant with a Spanish accent and two clean-cut youngsters. Ernie Soto was from Arizona and was six feet, eight inches tall. He was about 30 years old and had been with a sheriff's department in Arizona prior to entering the Border Patrol. He was a real bargain for Uncle Sam. About all he needed was to learn what we did and how we did it. He was already a seasoned officer. You did not have to worry about your back when he was along. He had played professional basketball all over Mexico under an assumed name so he could retain his eligibility to play college ball in the U.S. under a scholarship. He could recognize a Central American claiming to be Mexican in short order and everyone liked to work with him. Ernie was still working at Uvalde when I retired but, not too long after that, took a transfer, I believe, to Arizona. I have no doubt that he did well at anything he undertook.

The second was a young man named Robert Wilson. He was single and just out of college. I am sure he was a good student in the Academy. I thought he probably led a sheltered life at home. He was from around Yakima, Washington. He was green and needed seasoning. He was a dead shot with handguns, cleaned the course at the Academy, and, although I never saw the certificate, he should have had a distinguished masters rating. He had potential and, since he had made it through the academy, I thought he had a good chance to make probation.

It was during the cool season when they arrived. I started taking Robert to the brush with me as often as possible. We worked at the other operations also, but I wanted him to know something of the brush work before the hot summer arrived, as working the brush in the hottest part of the year was brutal. There were places in the brush country where a person unaccustomed to the area could have stayed lost for days. Bob never became a top notch sign cutter, but he was better than he thought he was and he never quit. This gained more respect for him than he knew. If he reads this, he will learn for the first time that he was not the worst sign cutter I ever worked with.

When I was in Eagle Pass, we got a trainee from Pittsburg. It was apparent that this young fellow had been raised on the concrete of the city streets and the concept of following someone by looking at the ground just did not register with him. Otherwise, he was a pretty good man, but could not see a track on the ground. When working with this fellow, I once stopped on a drag strip where a group of aliens had crossed and left a very clear sign. As a test, I waited until he had walked to the strip and was standing with a clear track right between his feet. I called his attention to it but he could not make it out. I kept trying to get him to see it and he finally said he did, but I could tell by the blank look in his eyes that he never saw it and just said he did to satisfy me.

Despite mistakes here and there, Bob was maturing as the year ended and he successfully completed his probationary year. He worked in the Uvalde station several years after I retired and finally transferred back to Washington. He had a successful career. I had lost contact with him until a few months ago, when I ran across my name on the internet and discovered he had retired after a 25 year career and was writing some of his memories of the Border Patrol. He had included his work with me in one of the stories. He is now a successful author and has one book that I know of in print. He also writes concerning immigration matters for a Spokane, Washington, newspaper.

The third trainee was Arnold "Skip" Buxton, who was raised in Rhode Island. He was also young, but was self-confident and had some understanding of the outdoors. He was a good prospect and, when faced with a problem, usually made the right decision. He was a fan of the New England Patriots—probably the only one in a hundred miles of Uvalde. He was engaged to a girl back home who was in school, learning to be a medical records specialist. They planned to be married as soon as she finished her classes.

One of the ranchers I had become friends with was on the

Board of Directors of the local hospital. I think I was the first, but not the only one, to talk to him about getting a job for her when she finished school. In any event, there was a job at the local hospital waiting for her when she arrived.

Skip and my son, David, had arrived only a month or so apart. They hit it off and were soon friends. They worked together often and made an outstanding team. When Skip's fiancée, Michele (we called her Ellie), arrived after graduating as a medical records specialist, we found she was a beautiful young woman with an outgoing personality. My wife was immediately moved to take Ellie under her wing. With the camaraderie and friendship between David and Skip, this young couple quickly became family. Skip and Ellie did well in Uvalde, and Skip was soon enrolled in pilot training school at our local college, continuing until he was a licensed pilot. We met Ellie's sister who visited from Rhode Island and, later, Skip's mother. Skip was one of the very best young officers I ever helped train. After he and Ellie stayed for a few years, he took a transfer to the Canadian border. When they left, it was much like a pair of children had left town. We maintained contact, with Sylvia sending them salsa and they sent us maple syrup at Christmas. Skip worked on the Canadian border in New Hampshire a couple of years or so then took a position as a State Police Officer back in Rhode Island.

The state of Rhode Island got a real bargain when they got Skip. He had to attend another academy, but I am sure he sailed through without problems. He was the only Spanish speaker in the force and was soon acting as translator for their court cases. As I write this, Skip is nearing retirement age and is a lieutenant in the Rhode Island State Police.

That was the year we had two on-duty deaths in our area law enforcement community. This should give an idea how easy it is for an officer to lose his life on duty and how vigilant an officer has to be to minimize the risks.

I have previously mentioned the rivers which head in the Texas Hill Country and run through Uvalde County. Ninety percent of the time they are clear, sedate, small streams and can be waded almost anywhere. Many of them are crossed by low water crossings which have galvanized metal tubes that carry the water underneath the roadway. However, after heavy rains in the Edwards Plateau area, they can become raging torrents, causing the water to run over the road as the tubes cannot carry all the water coming down the river. The road then becomes a weir dam and the lower side of these roads can become a death trap as anything or anyone going over the dam becomes trapped by the powerful undertow caused by the dam.

Not long after David had transferred to Uvalde, he worked with Sammie Stewart. They were on Highway 127 a few miles west of Sabinal. There had been heavy rains and water was spilling over the low water crossing on the Sabinal River. When they reached the crossing over Highway 127, they found road closed signs up and a heavy current in the river and water too deep to cross running across the highway. Someone (as someone usually does) had driven around the signs and tried to drive across the bridge in spite of the heavy flow across the road. He got stranded in the middle of the bridge and was in his car.

A rescue effort was under way and there was quite a group of spectators as a young officer from Sabinal was preparing to rescue the stranded motorist. The officer took a length of rope and, after putting on a life vest, entered the water upriver from the stranded vehicle and floated down to the car. His plan so far was working perfectly. He tied the rope around the stranded man, but instead of tying himself to the rope, he decided to just hold on to it and let the rest of the rescue team on the bank just pull them both to safety at the same time. When he gave the signal and the crew began to pull them, the current swept them both over the edge of the road and into the maelstrom below. The young officer lost his grip on the rope and was immediately caught in the undertow and pulled under the surface of the water. The stranded motorist was pulled to safety, but the officer was trapped.

David was young and a strong swimmer, and, following his first impulse, unbuckled his gun belt and tried to hand it to Sammie Stewart. That undertow would have drowned a hundred men as easily as it did the one who was trapped and Sammie knew it. He saved the life of one of his officers by threatening to tackle and hold David if he tried to enter that water. It is hard to stand by helpless and see a tragedy like that happen, but it would have been twice the tragedy if Stewart had not acted as he did. I am eternally grateful to him for saving my son.

The other death on duty was Chief Deputy Sheriff Clyde Hobbs. He had been with the Sheriff's Department for several years and was in the process of leaving to take other employment. I don't remember if this was his last day or his last week, but my understanding was that he had already given notice that he was leaving. It was nearing time for him to get off duty for the day and some five minutes prior to his leaving the office, a call came that some people were trying to sell some welding equipment suspected to be stolen. He took this last call and was successful in finding the car as it was leaving the area. He stopped the car a short distance out of Uvalde, and during this stop, he was somehow jumped and beaten to death on the side of the roadway. Three men were involved, and they abandoned their car and ran away.

Deputy Hobbs died sometime during the night after the attack. I became involved in the case the next morning when the Border Patrol was asked to help track the men who fled from the scene of the attack. By that time, the car had been traced and we found out the occupants were from Eagle Pass, Texas. One of the city police officers and I found tracks going across the field adjoining the highway. We followed these tracks about one-and-a-half miles as they made a loop and angled back toward town after they got about a mile from the highway.

We had found where they had approached a hunting blind and there I found a torn part of a pants leg. This piece of cloth had what appeared to be blood smears on it and was kept as evidence by the police officer who accompanied me. From the sign I found, I thought they had spent some time in or around the blind, possibly waiting for daylight to get their bearings. From the blind, they went into a subdivision where they walked down a gravel road over which traffic had obliterated the tracks. They could be followed no further. One of the other officers, in talking with area residents, found someone who had seen three men who he believed was them walking down the road toward town just after daylight that morning.

That was the end of my involvement in that case. I know road blocks were set up and manned for days afterward. My understanding was that the road blocks made it impossible for whoever was hiding them in town (if anyone was) to take them home by auto and, therefore, they tried to walk home. They were apprehended several days later north of Eagle Pass, Texas, forty miles from Uvalde by a team of Border Patrolmen. They were convicted and sentenced to life in prison.

★ Chapter Twenty-Seven ★

The very terrain in which we worked sometimes made operations difficult. I remember one instance in which I was working with a partner in farm and ranch operations. We were driving up Highway 83 toward Leakey, when James Banks called on the radio saying he was on Highway 55 just south of Camp Wood. Banks was a Texan from the Brownwood area and had transferred from Eagle Pass to Uvalde at the same time that I had. He had tried to stop a pickup with a camper and had pulled alongside the pickup and motioned for the driver to pull over. Instead of doing so, the driver had swerved the pickup into the utility vehicle that Banks was driving. He had hit Banks' vehicle hard enough to knock it completely off the pavement and into the bar ditch. The vehicle stayed upright and Banks came right back out, still in pursuit.

My partner and I were about ten miles south of Leakey and there was a road from Leakey to Camp Wood, but when the pursuit went through Camp Wood, it looked like we would have to go all the way to Highway 41 and cut across to Rock Springs to help. This was more than fifty miles and we would probably still be behind the chase. We decided to cut across at Leakey and get behind the chase at Camp Wood, although we would be far behind. It took us a while to drive to Camp Wood and we were fortunate that Banks was able to get the pickup stopped north of Camp Wood in the Barksdale area. He held the case intact on the highway until my partner and I got there, then we moved it back to Uvalde. The driver had got out of the pickup holding a Bible in front of his chest when Banks finally stopped him.

I later looked at the sign where the pickup had knocked the Border Patrol vehicle off the road. There was a chest high embankment where Banks had gone off the road. His vehicle had left the ground for a considerable distance and had landed upright. The embankment ended some distance ahead and Banks had done a neat piece of driving to keep upright and stay in pursuit. This typified the experience and know-how of the men in the Uvalde Station. It also shows just why I was so proud of the training that our trainees received when they came here from the academy.

I do not believe in second sight or clairvoyance. I am not a psychic and do not believe I have ever known anyone who was. Yet, I have seen things happen for which I have no explanation.

I was working along the railroad alone one day. I had seen some tracks in the Cline area of a couple of aliens traveling east and staying parallel to the railroad, but some one to two hundred yards distant. It was late and I was about ready to call it a day, but worked this pair on toward Uvalde. Some five miles from town, I finally spotted them in a pasture. I called for a plane to hold them and waited for him to arrive. When he had them hiding in the brush, I walked toward them and got within some 25 yards and called them to come out of the brush as they were caught and had no chance to escape from the plane. They stood up and started walking toward me and when they got within thirty feet, I told them to stop. I then told them if they had any knives, guns, or other weapons to put them on the ground. One put a small pocket knife on the ground the other took another step or two toward me and stopped as if he had no weapon. I immediately pointed my gun at him and told him to put it on the ground right there and right now. That got his attention and he dropped what I later found to be a razor sharp hunting knife with a six-inch blade. As I cuffed them and started walking toward my vehicle, I noticed a rancher whom I knew had been parked, watching the action. He started his vehicle and drove away.

I saw him in the coffee shop a few days later and he said something had been bothering him and could he ask me a question. Of course, I told him to go ahead. He asked me how I knew the man I arrested a few days prior had a knife. He had seen me suddenly draw the gun and point it at the alien. It was a legitimate question. I thought about it a minute and realized that I did not know how I knew the man was armed, but I had known. I told him that I just knew. That I could not say exactly how I knew,

I just knew. That is still true as I write this. I knew, but I don't know how I knew.

I was on a fishing trip with a couple of other fishermen and we had stopped at a truck stop in Fairfield, Texas, south of Dallas to get fuel and supplies. This was a busy place off Interstate 45 and there were probably 15 to 20 people scattered around the building. I noticed a well-dressed, middle-aged lady enter the store and look around. I was standing at a counter about the middle of the store and she spotted me and walked half way across the store past several other men.

She stopped in front of me and confidently asked, "Habla español?" She was looking for a small, nearby town and did not have a map and needed help. I was glad to help her get a map and tell her how to recognize the exit she needed to take. As she left, I noticed that she was driving a nice car with Mexico plates. How she happened to pick me out of all the other people in the store I still don't know, but from her manner when she asked me if I knew Spanish, she clearly expected an affirmative answer.

I remember when one spoken word probably saved a life. I was working along the railroad in the Cline area west of Uvalde and found fresh tracks of two men walking east toward Uvalde. Instead of following behind them, I got on nearby Highway 90, drove four miles east, and then cut through a ranch back to the railroad. I stopped and walked to the fence line and carefully looked back down the railroad. I made a good guess and saw the men walking down the access road one-half mile short of where I was. I waited until they were almost even with me before I stepped out in front of them. It was a hot summer day and they were tired. They did not try to run and looked peaceful enough, so I did not take any special precautions. I just asked them if they had any knives, guns, or other weapons prior to patting them down. One of them, who was wearing his shirt outside his belt, said in Spanish, "Just this toy," as he raised the hem of the shirt and pulled a gun out of his belt.

The word he used was "juguete." By the time the gun cleared his belt, my gun was pointed at him and I hesitated long enough to recognize that he was telling the truth just as he realized he had made a mistake and dropped the gun. At first glance, it certainly did not look like a toy. It probably scared me almost as badly as it did him. I would have found it hard to live with myself if I had shot a man who was just trying to hand me a toy.

As Sammie Stewart settled in to running the day-to-day operations of the Uvalde Border Patrol Station, it became the kind of station every trainee should have in which to gain experience and every journeyman should be proud to be a part of. We ran train checks in cooperation with the railroad detectives. We caught smuggling cases and seized vehicles. We did farm and ranch check the way it should be done. We worked the brush country and used confidential informants to make arrests that would have otherwise been missed. As more trainees were assigned to the station, we would take a large detention bus and driver, an aircraft, and a crew of men and sweep the building sites in the Hill Country including the Kerrville and Bandera areas. We kicked butt and took names. Jack Richardson, the Chief Patrol Agent of the Del Rio Sector, loved it. I remember one occasion when Chief Richardson flew as observer and went with us on one of these sweeps. We made him proud. During all this time, Sammie had our backs.

I was working near Leakey one day when two pickups passed us. One was a crew cab pulling a large horse trailer, the other had a young man and a passenger who I thought should be checked for citizenship. I told my trainee driver to pass the young man and his passenger and stop the one with the trailer. I intended to wave down the following pickup and check it also. The trainee did as requested and, while he was checking the front pickup, I stopped the one following, only to find that he had stopped and let his passenger escape before he came on around the curve which we had to pass to catch the lead truck. When I questioned the young fellow about the passenger he had unloaded, he was polite enough, but the smirk on his face betrayed just how proud he was of himself. I knew his father, a prominent rancher who lived up on the divide above Leakey, and now I knew the son.

About six weeks later, I was in the Hill Country again and drove up on an operation where cattle were being moved from a pasture on one side of the road to the other. Gates on both sides were open and I recognized this same young man and the fellow helping him sure looked like the man I had seen in his pickup a few weeks earlier. The employee had just tied his horse and walked away. I cut him off from the horse with my vehicle and, sure enough, he was the same man. I arrested him on the spot and the young man told me what a bind I was leaving him in. I was just as polite to him as he had been to me a few weeks earlier and probably just as pleased with myself as he had been. I left him with gates open on both sides of the road, cattle in both pastures, and the horse tied to the gate posts. There was virtually nothing but local traffic on this rural road and I was not worried about traffic hazards.

When I got to the office later that day, the rancher's Continental was parked in front and the rancher and Sammie were in conference in his office. After he had left, I asked Sammie what the rancher had said and Sammie told me he had said that I had been brusque with his son. To give the rancher credit, brusque was probably the most accurate term he could have used to describe my treatment of his son earlier that day. He apparently did not exaggerate as I had expected him to. I don't remember exactly what else was said but, in the end, I knew that if I had needed help all I would have had to do was let Sammie know. He had my back all the way and that was before he knew what the young man had done a few weeks prior.

★ Chapter Twenty-Eight ★

Buck Miller did not run for re-election in Real County. He took a job with the Texas Department of Safety as a Highway Patrolman and was stationed in Menard, Texas. The new Sheriff was a former Game Warden, and I continued to work with and get good cooperation from the Sheriff's Department in Leakey. I became involved in a case by virtue of being in the Sheriff's Office in Leakey one day when there was a mishap on Highway 83 a few miles north of town which resulted in the arrest of two occupants of a sports utility vehicle. I went with the Sheriff to the scene. The vehicle had run off the road, through a fence, but, except for some scratches, the car was not badly damaged. Upon searching the vehicle, we found several empty plastic trash bags, which contained what we believed to be marijuana residue.

The Sheriff called the wrecker service and had the vehicle towed and stored. When we returned to the office, we found the two men, who had occupied the vehicle, held a considerable amount of money on their persons. Their pockets were full of packets of bills and they had even shoved packets in their boots. I don't remember the final amount, but it was several thousand dollars. The money was seized along with the vehicle.

I had nothing to do with the case until the court date. I had not been subpoenaed, but was on hand at the courthouse in case I was needed as a witness. When I arrived at the Sheriff's Office, there was considerable activity. I was told the District Attorney was in the judge's chambers with the judge and the attorney for the defendants, trying to arrange a plea bargain. The Sheriff was trying to get a word to the District Attorney without the court or defense knowing about it. Seizure proceedings had been filed against both the money and the stored vehicle. That morning, someone from the Sheriff's Office had gone to the lot where the seized car had been stored to check about getting it ready in case they lost the seizure case and had to return the vehicle to the defendant.

There was some consternation around the office because the vehicle had been found scattered over a hundred feet of the lot, having been cut to pieces. It seemed the wrecker operator's wife was a member of the Leakey EMS, and they had recently obtained a Jaws of Life tool. She had asked him to give them a vehicle out of the lot on which to practice. He had told her which vehicle to use but she misunderstood. They had really done a job on the wrong car. The sheriff had not been able to get word to the District Attorney and everyone had their fingers crossed. When the District Attorney finally emerged from the judge's chambers, he had a plea bargain arranged and the seizure of the vehicle had been agreed to and it belonged to the County of Real. A collective sigh of relief went through the Sheriff's Office. I'm sure the wrecker operator was even more relieved.

Although I was now spending a considerable amount of time in the Hill Country, I had not abandoned the brush country and spent as much time as I could there. One day, I had been working with Mack Porter in the southwest area of the county and we were nearing the end of the shift. As we drove toward Uvalde, Mack drove through a rural subdivision just outside Uvalde. The area was subdivided into small acreages and contained all manner of residences. As we approached one place, we could see workers in the backyard and stopped to check them.

There were four illegal aliens who were building a watering trough of concrete and setting some posts. The owner was raising goats in a small pasture behind the house. They had built a wooden trough of 2 x 12 boards, roughly 10 feet long, and mixed concrete in it. Then, they used a wheelbarrow to move concrete to the molds for the water trough and post holes. They had just finished mixing a new batch of concrete. One of the men was walking back and forth along the trough, stirring it with a hoe to keep it from hardening. When we arrested them, we learned the owner of the place had gone to Eagle Pass. Among other things, he had taken their Mexican money and was going to exchange it for U.S. money. They had no idea when he would return.

We had a bus which came from sector each day to pick up

processed aliens and haul them back to the border or to detention in Del Rio, depending upon the circumstances in the case. These aliens we just arrested would be returned to Mexico, and as we had stopped at this place, we heard the detention officer check 10-8 from Brackettville, in route to Uvalde. We knew we had about 45 minutes to get these people to the office and get them processed or we would have to haul them to the border ourselves. We took their names and asked them for an address to which the employer could mail anything he owed them. After some discussion, they decided to have the money sent to their local radio station.

We often had to leave names and addresses like this, but this was the only time during my career that an alien or group of aliens wanted their money mailed to a radio station. We left the information for the employer and started towards the office. Mack was driving and as he pulled onto the road, he looked at me and said, "Ken, I sure hope that fellow wants a big rock in his backyard." I assured him the man would be proud of it since it would be the only one in the neighborhood with a hoe handle sticking out of it.

I was raised in rural southern Oklahoma and nicknames were common. I remember Jay Bird Reeves, Cat Newberry, Peg (leg) Smith, Heel Fly Cannon, Toots Plaster, and others. Nicknames were also common in the Law enforcement community. Some were given by other officers, and it was not uncommon for a Border Patrolman to become well enough known by the illegals to be given a nickname by them. My son, Steven, who began his Border Patrol career in Laredo, became known among the aliens who crossed that area as El Nopal (Prickly Pear). He wore a well-trimmed mustache that was the color of the small golden stickers, which grow in small clumps on the prickly pears. Late in my career, I became known as El Indio (the Indian) by the numerous aliens I had apprehended. This was picked up by the men in my station. I have no idea what prompted this nickname or who or which group bestowed it. Although I do not know where my nickname started, I do know where at least one other did.

A man from New Mexico was stationed in the Del Rio sector. He was a fine Border Patrolman and somewhat of a practical joker. He once castigated a fellow agent who hit a roadrunner with the vehicle. The agent did not stop, and since the roadrunner was his state bird, he claimed he wanted to give it a state funeral.

The New Mexico native was working one day and during the operation, he was bitten by a dog. Nothing serious, but his fellow agents lost no time in giving him the nickname Alpo. It stuck and he was thereafter known throughout the sector and beyond as Alpo.

★ Chapter Twenty-Nine ★

Everyone has seen the high-speed chase where the young punk endangers numerous other drivers trying to escape from pursuing officers. Then, after he wrecks his vehicle, he jumps out, runs until caught and physically subdued after fighting, biting and kicking the officers. He spits in the face of one as they put him in the cruiser after finally being handcuffed, all the while calling the officers every vile name he knows, and he knows plenty. The officers stoically endure his abuse without retaliation.

Later, you learn the officers have been investigated and the agency they work for is being sued because the punk's lawyer claims the officers used excessive force in arresting the man. Unless there is video of the arrest and the man's resistance, these cases sometimes end with the punk going free and his lawyer smiling all the way to the bank.

I was involved in a few of these arrests but was fortunate I was never sued or accused of excessive force. There were a few times in my career that I responded to situations that tended to suggest I might be human rather than a robot the public expects us to be.

It was a hot summer day and not a breath of air was stirring. I had been working alone in the brush all day and was driving back to Uvalde without having made any arrests. A group of seven aliens ran across the road a few hundred yards ahead of me and I began to attempt to take them into custody. They were walking parallel to a power line which ran toward Uvalde. There was a large hill near the power line a mile past where I had seen the aliens. Rather than trying to overtake them, I chose to drive to the hill and climb high enough to see the area I expected them to cross as they continued east toward Uvalde. The aliens did not come when they should have; therefore, I knew they were stopped in a draw nearby because I could see everything else.

I started walking back up the draw, expecting them to be laid up somewhere within a half mile or so. I walked up the draw two or three hundred yards when I saw the aliens through the brush walking toward me. I immediately dropped behind a bush only to discover I had landed on my stomach with a large leaf of prickly pear squarely under my midsection. I could not move without risk of being seen so I waited until the aliens walked up close. I was in their midst before they could react. I picked who I thought was the leader and his helper and handcuffed them together. The others followed as we walked back to my vehicle. I noticed them muttering under their breath and discovered they believed I had stuck the pear leaf to my uniform as camouflage.

I put them in the back of my utility vehicle and was driving toward Uvalde when an oil well service pickup passed me. One of the occupants pointed to the rear wheel on my side. I was nearing a bridge where it would be dangerous to change a tire, so I shut my vehicle down and, as expected, found the tires all aired and nothing wrong. I got back in and followed the pickup, catching up with it about the time we reached town.

Knowing where their offices were, I knew where they would make a right turn up ahead. When they slowed for the turn, I cut across the parking lot of a restaurant, stepped out in front of them, and waved them down. I told the fellow who had signaled me that I had seen his signal, and found nothing wrong and wanted to know what the signal was for. Again, as expected, he said he just wanted to let me know the wheel was rolling. I thanked him for the information and told him as long as we were doing signals, I had one for him. I gave him the signal I thought the occasion called for and stepped back to give him room to get out of his vehicle. His face turned red, and he half-choked but was still sitting there when the driver pulled away.

Mack Porter and I had been working in the Hill Country. We were following up on a lead that illegal aliens were being used in a cedar cutting operation and were looking for the location. Mack was driving and parked our vehicle at the foot of a steep hill. We walked to the top to look over the country and see if we were in the right location. There had been some activity there, but no one was there at that time.

Mack started back to the vehicle before me and was 30 to 40

yards ahead when he reached the car. A pickup had parked near our vehicle and, as I got closer, I could hear raised voices. I expected it was the ranch manager. Even though I had never met the man, I got a clue that we might not become bosom buddies when I heard him tell Mack, "Well, y'all sure are stupid." He kept expanding on this theme, and the closer I got, the less I liked what I was hearing. By the time I approached them, he was really getting wound up. I interrupted him, telling him it was clear he was just looking for an excuse to raise hell. I invited him to just cut his wolf loose and let me see just how bad he was. This was not in the script he had written for this scene and was taken aback. When he got his breath, he assured me we would see about that. Whatever it was we were going to see about, it was not right then and there. So, Mack and I went on about our business.

I never heard a word from my people about this, but a few days later a Deputy Sheriff was smiling and telling me that a man had been in and talked to the Sheriff. The Deputy heard my name and the man said, "He can't talk like that to me, can he?" And the Sheriff, ever the politician, said, "Well, he sure shouldn't."

I don't believe I talked to this man again, but the next time I remember his name came up was when a Criminal Investigator came to our office looking for someone to show him where this ranch was and help him find this man. One of the other Patrolmen went with him, but later told me the investigator had statements from aliens that had been picked up further inland who said they had been put on a plane by this ranch manager and a pilot flew them to another ranch in a state further inland. I am not sure if an alien smuggling case was ever made on this or not.

Sammie Stewart decided to climb another rung up the career ladder and accepted a promotion. He left Uvalde to move to Arizona. We were, again, without a Patrol Agent in Charge, and the Senior Patrol Agent was acting as Patrol Agent in Charge, running the day-to-day operations of the station. Although we were having trainees assigned to us out of the academy, the station continued to operate without much change. Shortly thereafter, a supervisory officer was transferred to Uvalde from a station in New Mexico, which was primarily a traffic check station. He was a nice enough fellow, but I always had the feeling he would have felt more comfortable in a station which did more traffic check. I do not believe he was comfortable trying to supervise the freewheeling group of men we had at the Uvalde station.

There was a brief period of confusion as to who was in charge of the station because we had a supervisory officer but also an agent who had been designated as acting Patrol Agent in Charge. This was soon straightened out in sector with the supervisory agent being placed in charge of the station, but, to the best of my memory, he was never the official Patrol Agent in Charge of the station. He just took over as acting as the figurehead Patrol Agent in Charge.

It was during this time that I was working in the Hill Country and as I drove from Camp Wood toward Leakey on Highway 337, my vehicle was passed by a van. An adult driver and passenger were visible in the front seats and two or three young people were in the seats behind them, but in the back there were several people who appeared to be aliens.

I pulled the van over. The driver said he was coming from a Boy Scout camp above Camp Wood and was taking a man to a clinic in Leakey. The men in the back of the van were aliens from Mexico who had illegally entered the United States. He may have been taking a man to the clinic, but there were four aliens and they all did not need to go to a clinic. I knew he was furthering their entry into the U.S. I took his driver's license, put the aliens in my vehicle, and followed him to Uvalde. I led him to the office and unloaded the vehicle.

I notified the office that I was bringing the vehicle in and gave them the license number, and I believe I was asked for and gave the name on the driver's license. Upon arriving at the office, I moved the aliens inside and prepared to question them about the details of the case. The supervisor took the driver into his office. I then talked to the supervisor and learned he was a prominent banker in Del Rio, was well-known to the supervisor, and had good standing in his community and Del Rio. I also learned he had called someone in the prosecutions office, and they already decided there would be no prosecution. This was the first and only case during my career that was declined so precipitously.

★ Chapter Thirty ★

I can't think of any profession that had to deal with more hypocrisy than the Border Patrol, except possibly some ministers. This was especially true with farm and ranch check. When we apprehended an alien or a group of aliens who were employed, the first order of business was to gather up their clothes and other belongings. This entailed a trip to whatever living quarters were furnished. If it was a farm or ranch, it was usually an old farm house or an unused outbuilding of some kind, although it was not uncommon to find them living in a tent or lean-to. I soon learned that by looking in the refrigerator, when there was one, I could learn what kind of employer with whom we would be dealing. If I found a well-stocked refrigerator, more often than not, the employer treated them well and paid them at least part of what their labor was worth.

All too often this was not the case. I remember one man in the Hill Country who dealt in cedar posts and usually had a crew somewhere in the area. They were hard to find, but, when found, they would usually be camped and conditions would be primitive. When they were taken to collect their wages, payday would be Tuesday, Thursday, or someday other than the present day. We always left their names and addresses to which he could mail the wages. Our suspicions were confirmed one night when one of the Border Patrolmen got a call from this fellow and he was scared. He said his yard was full of people who said he owed them money, and they were not going to leave until they got their money. He wanted the Border Patrolman to come and arrest them. My understanding was he told the man to pay them what he owed them, and if they were still there in the morning, call back and he would come check their citizenship.

In another instance, I was working with a partner and we found three or four men who appeared to be aliens working around the house of a well-known and respected rancher in the Camp Wood area. We checked with these men who proved to be illegally in the country. We gathered their baggage together and went to the ranch house to collect their wages. The rancher was apparently gone, but his wife came to the door. When we told her we were bringing her hands to collect their wages, she gave us both a good dressing down for taking these poor people, who were not hurting anything, and had just come to this country to earn money to feed their starving families and on and on. She finally got around to paying them for the five days each of them had worked on the ranch. This paragon of philanthropy gave each of them five dollars.

In the meantime, the Uvalde station got a new Patrol Agent in Charge. He was Billy Kring, who transferred to Uvalde from the Comstock station. He was a local man and knew the area and many of the people of the county. He was another winner for the station. He ran the station much like Sammie Stewart had and with much of the same results. He was a leader by example. Billy was an active participant in the field work and did a full share. I don't remember ever hearing anyone in the station complain about the support they got from him. By this time, David LaMascus and Skip Buxton were working in the Hill Country as a team and having good results in making smuggling cases. They were having chases of fleeing vehicles where they would sometimes have to call ahead to the Police Department in Kerrville to get assistance in stopping the chase.

Billy would often work another part of the Hill Country with Ernie Soto, and they were having equal success in their area. Between these two teams, they had people who hauled aliens through the Hill Country looking over their shoulders. These areas were on the edge of the radio range capabilities and communication was iffy and sometimes nonexistent. The Border Patrol vehicles were stock while many of the smugglers had spent a lot of money making their vehicles fast. This was tough, dangerous work and made for some interesting situations. Men had to know what they were doing and how to do it.

One of the routes most traveled by aliens in our area had been used more frequently. I located the point where the road funneled through a canyon in the Hill Country near Concan, twenty miles north of Uvalde. I talked about a camping detail on this trail with the station supervisor, Kring, and told him what the sign indicated about the number of people we could reasonably expect to apprehend on a five-day camping detail. He agreed and obtained approval and funds from sector headquarters.

This was to be a four-man detail but one man got sick at the last minute. Also, we had just been notified the water discharge from Amistad dam had increased to the point where it was impossible for aliens to cross the river in the area where the trail began. Since the detail had already been approved, sector wanted it held even if I didn't think it would be productive. I pulled a small two man camper and set it up along with a tent at the site. We spent the first afternoon and night there and, just as expected, not a single alien walked down the trail.

I decided not to let the detail be a failure. We were in plain clothes and had an unmarked vehicle. We went far and wide, apprehending aliens right and left before they realized we were Border Patrolmen. We apprehended more aliens than I originally estimated, thus having a successful detail instead of a failure. I don't know why sector insisted we hold an operation that was sure to fail. I do know if someone else requests a camping detail to that area, they will not be able to look back at the records and deny permission. During the five days we camped on that trail, a total of three aliens came down the trail.

A few days after the detail ended, the water discharge at the dam was reduced to normal. I gave it three days, then went back by myself to the same spot we had camped and caught all the aliens I could haul back to Uvalde and lost many more than I caught. Within a three mile stretch of that trail, I found four groups of aliens. It was getting dark and I did not get a good count, but there were more than 30 aliens just in that three mile section of the trail.

Although we now had more agents stationed in Uvalde due to trainees being sent directly from the academy, Billy recognized they were being trained by journeymen who were giving them the kind of experience they needed in order to reach their full potential. During his tenure as Patrol Agent in Charge, the station had as many as 18 men, and the station continued to be the most productive in the sector, specifically in arrests per man hour. We continued sweeps through the construction sites in the Hill Country. To this day, I am proud to have been part of this operation. We did it like it should have been done with great support from our Patrol Agent in Charge.

Around this time, there was an incident which we in the Uvalde station apparently took more seriously than anyone else. My son, David, was checking a train in the Cline area when an alien ran from him. He ran the man down and stopped him some distance away. Since he could not get away by running, he tried to take David's pistol and a lengthy tussle ensued with the alien making repeated attempts to get the gun. He was strong and David had to use both hands to keep possession of the weapon. Enough finally became enough with David and he put the muzzle of the gun in the guy's ear and made it clear that he was about to hear the last sound he would ever hear. He finally gave up and was arrested. He had been with a group and someone else had arrested the remainder of the group.

The man was processed for prosecution. I remember telling his companions, who were going to be returned to Mexico that day, that this man would not be going with them, and it would be some time before they might hear from him. I did not do the paperwork on the man but remember someone saying he was claiming to be only 16 years old. Even if this was true, there were federal facilities for juveniles. Since it was common practice for many aliens to claim to be juveniles in order to avoid responsibility for their actions, I doubted his claim. He did not look like a juvenile.

We sent him to sector, fully expecting him to be prosecuted either as an adult or, if he was, in fact, a juvenile, then as a juvenile. I don't believe anyone in our office believed he would not have shot David if he had successfully gotten possession of the gun. I was disappointed and disgusted to learn a few days later that whoever had been responsible for handling this case had dealt with it as any other juvenile case, and sent him back to Mexico with the rest of his group.

★ Chapter Thirty-One ★

I was in the office one day when an FBI Agent out of San Antonio came to our office and handed me a paper saying a certain affair did not even justify investigation by one agent much less two. He handed me a paper and left before I could open and read it. Upon reading the paper, I found it was a notice that the FBI would take no further action in a certain matter. It gave a name, and after thinking about it a minute, I figured out what it was all about. Some two or three weeks prior, a group of aliens were apprehended and were being processed in the office. One of the aliens and one of the Border Patrolmen had gotten into some kind of disagreement just before I had entered the building.

I was helping process the aliens, and I got one out of the detention area, brought him forward, and began processing him. One of the other guys in the office remarked that this was the man with whom one of the other men had an argument. I went ahead and processed him without thinking anything else about it. Apparently the argument had ended with the man shoved up against a wall, or something similar, and the FBI had received some kind of complaint. It must have been minor. As to my knowledge, no one in our office had been questioned about this matter.

Apparently, the FBI had talked to whoever the complainant was and decided there was nothing further to investigate. They just looked at the paperwork and delivered the notice of no action taken to the person whose name appeared on the paperwork. I like to think that if they had found a violation, they would have asked the complainant if the same man who processed him was the man with whom he had the fuss. Since whatever it was had been settled and was over with, I did not take it any further.

One of the last criminal cases I made as a U.S. Border Patrol Agent is one which I believe is much more widespread than is generally known and which does not receive nearly enough attention from the federal and state governments. Political correctness is making it difficult to prevent this violation of our laws or to get effective prosecution of the laws on the books. Activist organizations and courts are also making it difficult to pass and enforce effective legislation.

I was working in the Uvalde area one day and a young man came to my attention. I don't remember exactly what he did, but I stopped him and checked his citizenship. He was a Mexican citizen, but was a legal resident of the United States and lived in Uvalde with his family. I asked to see his immigration card, and he took his wallet out of his pocket and produced his card. In the process, I noticed he also had what looked like a voter registration card in his wallet and asked him. He said it was his, and he had voted in the democratic primary, which had been held a few weeks previously.

Although he was a legal resident, lawfully admitted to live here, he was not a citizen and was not entitled to vote or to register to vote. I told him this and seized the voter registration card with the intention of notifying the FBI, which had jurisdiction over this particular violation. The card did indeed have a stamp indicating he had already used the card and voted in the democratic primary. Bright and early the next morning, he arrived at our office with his mother who had brought him in to see how much trouble he was in. I had intended to turn the case over to the FBI at the point I had left the day before, but inasmuch as Mama had brought him in voluntarily, I gave the Miranda warning and took a statement from him with Mama present. He stated he had been recruited to register to vote by some local men who helped him with the paper work. They had gone with him to the courthouse and filed the papers for him after which he had been given the registration card.

I had time that afternoon so I went to the County Court house and clerk's office. The county records showed he had submitted an application for voter registration, claiming to have been naturalized by a district court in North Dakota and given a naturalization case number on the registration application. I talked to the clerk and was informed that she required only a social security number to approve an application for voter registration.

Apparently, no attempt at verification had been made as to the naturalization. I did not learn if any documentation was submitted with the application. I submitted a cover letter with the Statement. This was all done shortly before I retired. A few weeks after I retired, my son, David, said an FBI Agent had asked him to relay to me that this turned out to be a big case. I never heard anything further about this matter and do not know the final outcome.

I was 37 years old when I entered the U.S. Border Patrol which was the law enforcement section of the Immigration and Naturalization Service. Sometime after my entry, the age limit at which the Border Patrol would accept applications was changed to thirty five years and mandatory retirement was age 55. Since I would have only some 18 years of service when I reached age 55, I was given an automatic extension until I completed 20 years of service.

I knew the exact date of my retirement for years beforehand and this gave me time to arrange my affairs. By the time April 30, 1987, arrived, I had my home and vehicles paid for and was ready for retirement. I was an avid fisherman of both fresh and salt water. I had bought welding equipment and equipped my shop with the intention of buying and selling used boats and motors, thus supplementing my retirement income by combining my favorite hobby with business.

It was a rare Border Patrolman who would pass up the chance at a party and the members of the Uvalde Station were no exception. My retirement celebration was held at the home of my friend and fellow Border Patrol agent Don Butler. Don was a Texan, originally from the Plainview area on the high plains. He had come to Uvalde from upstate New York some three years after I came from Eagle Pass. He was an outstanding Border Patrolman and, in his spare time, a fine craftsman working with either wood or metal. We never worked a lot together, I think, primarily because we both liked to work alone and were usually in different areas of our territory. When help was needed, Don would be right there and would stay as long as needed. He did his full share and was a credit to the Patrol. Don retired a few years after I did. He still lives in Uvalde and I see him around town from time to time.

My retirement party was not a large affair and was the way I liked it. Don's place had a big backyard and there was plenty of room for everyone. The Chief Patrol Agent and Deputy Chief were there from Del Rio. Sammie Stewart came and both my Agent sons were also there as were my other two children. Also in attendance were highway patrolmen, policemen, people from the Sheriff's Department, a couple of pilots, and a couple of detectives from the railroad. Altogether probably 50 to 65 people showed up. Food was eaten, beer was consumed, photos were taken, some nice things were said, a couple of which might even have been true. Billy Kring presented me one of the latest models of Eagle Fish Finders and Sylvia got an apron full of Susan B. Anthony coins for putting up with me all those years.

Son Steven was now stationed in Brackettville, but still had his friends in Laredo and had called in a few favors. He had gotten his old buddies in Laredo to find and seize a car hood boat which he gleefully had carried out from where it was hidden and presented to me. A car hood boat was made by taking two hoods from old cars, turning them back to back and welding them together, making a double end boat. The boat was propelled by oars made from two-by-fours with a piece of plywood nailed to the end which went into the water. Almost every town along the border had one or more of these operated by an enterprising resident to haul people across the river for a fee and land them to avoid both the Border Patrol and danger of drowning. These boatmen were wily as coyotes and hard to catch. Steve laughed and said if they had all the money they had spent in man hours to catch this one, they could have bought me a new Ranger. A good time was had, and it was a fitting end to a career of 30 years in investigations and law enforcement.

I recently asked my son, David, who is now Patrol Agent in Charge of the Uvalde Station, his opinion of the time when the present generation of Border Patrolmen consider where the old patrol ends and the present patrol begins. I thought he would probably say when the Border Patrol became part of Homeland

Security. He surprised me by saying he thought it would be about the time the revolver was replaced by the semi-automatic as the side arm issued to Border Patrolmen. The revolver was discontinued in 1994 and the Immigration and Naturalization Service became part of Homeland Security in 2003.

As my retirement neared, it was a time of rapid transition for the Border Patrol. Computers were installed in the stations, but programs for using them were still in the development stage. I was so close to retirement that I never used a computer in processing the paperwork for removal of an illegal alien from the United States. Women were being hired as Border Patrol Agents and there were a few in sector, but none were stationed in Uvalde. I did work a few times with a female partner, but only during train check operations when they were detailed to Uvalde for the train check operation. Items like GPS and cell phones were still in the future when I retired on April 30, 1987.

Even though it may be difficult to pick an exact date when the Old Patrol ended and the new began, I believe all would agree that I was a member of what is now known as the Old Patrol.